Becoming a
Critical Thinker

fifth edition

Becoming a
Critical Thinker

Vincent Ryan Ruggiero

HOUGHTON MIFFLIN COMPANY

Boston   New York

Publisher, Humanities: Patricia A. Coryell
Senior Sponsoring Editor: Mary Finch
Development Editor: Shani Fisher
Editorial Associate: Andrew Sylvester
Senior Project Editor: Fred Burns
Editorial Assistant: Brett Pasinella
Manufacturing Coordinator: Carrie Wagner
Senior Art and Design Coordinator: Jill Haber
Senior Composition Buyer: Sarah Ambrose
Marketing Manager: Elinor Gregory
Marketing Assistant: Evelyn Yang

Printed in the U.S.A.

Library of Congress Control Number: 2005920177

ISBN: 0-618-52783-4

6 7 8 9—CW—09 08 07

Acknowledgments

Many people have contributed to the fifth edition of this book. I would like to thank Fred Burns, project editor, Jill Haber, art and design coordinator, and Sarah Ambrose, composition buyer. My special thanks to Shani Fisher, development editor of Houghton Mifflin.

I also wish to acknowledge the contributions of the following professors, whose advice has been of great help to me in preparing this and/or previous editions of the book:

Marcia Anderson, Metropolitan State University (MN)

Robert Arend, San Diego Miramar College (CA)

Judy Bowie, DeVry University (IL)

Joel R. Brouwer, Montcalm Community College (MI)

Susan F. Corl, Louisiana State University, Eunice (LA)

Marilyn Corzine, Southwest Florida College of Business (FL)

Ozzie Dean, DeVry Institute of Technology, West Hills (CA)

Kathleen J. Fitzgerald, Columbia College (MO)

Catherine Gann, Missouri Western State College (MO)

Glennon Graham, Columbia College, Chicago (IL)

Fran Gray, Southwest Florida College of Business (FL)

Gail Herring, McLennan Community College (TX)

Melvin A. Jenkins, Indiana University of Pennsylvania (PA)

Martha Johnson, Texas A&M University (TX)

John Kowalczyk, Ferris State University (MI)

Patsy Krech, The University of Memphis (TN)

Cynthia H. LaBonne, Fairleigh Dickinson University (NJ)

Carol E. Lacey, Metropolitan State University (MN)

Nancy L. LaChance, DeVry Institute of Technology, Phoenix (AZ)

Joe LeVesque, Northwood University (TX)

Hakim J. Lucas, Medgar Evers College (NY)

Evelyn Martinez, Pima Community College—Desert Vista Campus (AZ)

Louise L. Myers, Naugatuck Valley Community College (CT)

Linda J. Nelson, Davenport University (IN)

Sharon Occipinti, Florida Metropolitan University—Tampa (FL)

Mary O'Shaughnessy, DeVry Institute of Technology, Long Beach (CA)

Jim Pollard, Spokane Falls Community College (WA)

Diane Rielly, Naugatuck Valley Community College (CT)

Margie Robertson, Manatee Community College (FL)

Anita Rosenfield, DeVry Institute of Technology, Pomona (CA)

Marni Sanft, Utah Valley State College (UT)

Penny Schempp, Western Iowa Tech Community College (IA)

Matt Schulte, Montgomery College (MD)

Andrew Scoblionko, DeVry Institute of Technology (NJ)

Karen Sookram, Doane College (NE)

Jeffrey D. Swanberg, Rockford Business College (IL)

Eric Sun, Macon State College (GA)

Mary Vacca, Briarcliffe College (NY)

Lynn E. Walker, Katherine Gibbs School, New York City (NY)

Joyce White, Mayville State University (ND)

Sheri L. Yarbrough, Kennedy-King College (IL)

Contents

Acknowledgments   v
To the Instructor   xiii

Introduction: Strategies for Effective Learning xv

Good Thinking! *The Story of Frank and Lillian Gilbreth xv*
    Plan your days   xvi
Good Thinking! *The Story of Art Fry xvi*
    View frustrations as opportunities   xvi
    Tackle unpleasant tasks immediately   xvii
    Chip away at big jobs   xviii
    Take charge of your mind   xviii
    Listen actively   xix
    Refuse to tolerate confusion   xix
    Study efficiently   xix
    Capture insights   xx
    Read for understanding   xx
    Keep a journal   xxi
    Turn these strategies into habits   xxi

1 Fundamentals of Thinking 1

What is intelligence?   2
Good Thinking! *The Story of Albert Einstein 3*
What is thinking?   4
Key principles of thinking   5
    Truth is discovered, not created   5
    A statement can't be both true and false at the same time
        and in the same way   7
    All people make mistakes, even experts   9
Good Thinking! *The Story of Elizabeth Loftus 10*
    Ideas can be examined without being embraced   11
    Feeling is no substitute for thinking   11
Identifying facts and opinions   12
Checking facts and testing opinions   15
    Consult everyday experience   17
    Consider the opinion's likely consequences   17
    Consider the implications   17
    Think of exceptions   18
    Think of counterexamples   18
    Reverse the opinion   19
    Look for relevant research   19

Evaluating evidence   21
Dare to change your mind   24
Good Thinking! *The Story of Stanton Samenow* 24
A comprehensive thinking strategy   26
    Step 1: Identify facts and opinions   27
    Step 2: Check the facts and test the opinion(s)   27
    Step 3: Evaluate the evidence   27
    Step 4: Make your judgment   27
Quiz   30

2 | Persuasive Communication 31

What is persuasion?   32
    Opportunities in the classroom   33
    Opportunities in the workplace   33
    Opportunities in the community   34
    Opportunities in relationships   34
How is persuasion achieved?   35
    Respect your audience   35
    Understand your audience's viewpoint(s)   35
    Begin on a point of agreement   35
Good Thinking! *The Story of Dale Carnegie 36*
    Acknowledge unpleasant facts and make appropriate
        concessions   36
    Apply the Golden Rule   37
    Keep your expectations modest   37
Strategy for persuasive writing   38
    Step 1: State what you think about the issue
        and why you think it   38
    Step 2: Consider how those who disagree might
        react to your view   39
    Step 3: Arrange your ideas and write a draft of your
        presentation   39
    Step 4: Check your draft for matters of style   40
    Step 5: Check your draft for grammar, usage,
        punctuation, and spelling   40
Good Thinking! *The Story of George Orwell 41*
Overcoming errors in grammar   42
    Make your subjects and predicates agree   42
    Choose correct pronoun case   42
    Avoid sentence fragments   43
    Avoid mixed constructions   43
    Make pronoun reference clear and accurate   44

Distinguish adverbs from adjectives   44
Choose proper comparatives and superlatives   44
Overcoming errors in usage   45
Strategy for persuasive speaking   47
Step 4: Create note cards 47
Step 5: Rehearse using a tape or video recorder   48
Strategy for group discussion   49
Quiz   55

3 | Becoming an Individual 57

What is individuality?   58
Good Thinking! *The Story of Viktor Frankl 59*
Acknowledging influences   59
Understanding attitudes   61
Four empowering attitudes   66
Attitude 1: There's always room for improvement   66
Attitude 2: Criticism, including self-criticism,
has value   67
Attitude 3: Effort is the key to success   67
Attitude 4: Other people are as important as I am   68
Recognizing manipulation   69
Biased reporting   69
Dishonest appeals to emotion   70
Stacking the deck   71
Suppressing dissent   71
Repetition   72
Resisting manipulation   72
Step 1: Be prepared   72
Step 2: Ask questions   73
Step 3: Be imaginative   75
Good Thinking! *The Story of Nellie Bly 77*
Step 4: Check sources   78
Habits for individuality   79
Be wary of first impressions   79
Be honest with yourself   80
Fight confusion   80
Produce many ideas   80
Acknowledge complexity   82
Look for connections among subjects   82
Consider other viewpoints   82
Base your judgment on evidence   83
Quiz   86

4 **Evaluating Arguments 87**

What is an argument?   88
Conducting library research   89
Good Thinking! *The Melvil Dewey Story 90*
Conducting Internet research   91
   Use a search engine   91
   Develop a resource list   91
Conducting an interview   94
Avoiding plagiarism   95
Revisiting evidence   97
   Anecdotes and cases-in-point   97
   Published reports   98
   Eyewitness testimony   98
   Expert testimony   98
Good Thinking! *The Story of Walter Reed 99*
   Experiments   100
   Statistical studies   100
   Surveys   100
   Research reviews   100
Evaluating complex arguments   101
   Step 1: Identify facts and opinions   101
   Step 2: Check the facts and test the opinions   104
   Step 3: Conduct research   105
   Step 4: Evaluate the evidence   105
   Step 5: Make your judgment   107
A caution about bias   107
Quiz   116

5 **Recognizing Errors in Thinking 117**

Three kinds of errors   118
Errors of perception   118
   "Mine is better" thinking   118
   Selective perception   119
   Gullibility and skepticism   119
Good Thinking! *The Story of Paul Vitz 120*
   Bias   121
   Pretending to know   122
   Either/or thinking   122
Errors of judgment   123
   Double standard   123
   Irrelevant criterion   124
   Overgeneralizing or stereotyping   124
Good Thinking! *The Story of Carol Tavris 125*
   Hasty conclusion   126
   Unwarranted assumption   126

Failure to make a distinction   128
Oversimplification   129
Errors of reaction   134
Explaining away   134
Shifting the burden of proof   134
Attacking the person   135
Straw man   135
Errors can multiply   138
Quiz   143

6 Applying Your Thinking Skills 145

Thinking critically about everyday problems   146
Step 1: Be alert for problems   147
Step 2: Express the problem   147
Step 3: List possible solutions   148
Step 4: Select and refine your best solution   148
Thinking critically about relationships   150
Good Thinking! The Story of Aaron Feuerstein 152
Guidelines for successful relationships   153
Thinking critically about careers   156
A sensible approach   158
Thinking critically about ethical judgments   159
A better basis for judgment   162
Good Thinking! The Story of Chiara Lubich 163
Applying the criteria   164
A sample case   164
Thinking critically about commercials   167
Bandwagon   168
Glittering generality   168
Empty comparison   168
Meaningless slogan   168
Testimonial   169
Transfer   169
Stacking the deck   169
Misleading statement   170
Thinking critically about print advertising   172
Thinking critically about television programming   175
Thinking critically about movies   182
Characters   183
Setting   183
Plot   183
Theme   183
Thinking critically about music   185
Thinking critically about magazines   187

Thinking critically about newspapers   190
Thinking critically about the Internet   193
    Whose site is this?   193
    What function does the site serve?   193
    Which statements are fact and which are opinion?   193
    Where can statements of fact be confirmed?   194
    How widely shared is this opinion? What do authorities
        on the subject think of it?   194
    Is the reasoning behind the opinion logical?   194
    Does the evidence support the opinion?   195
Quiz   196

Epilogue   199
Make the end a beginning   199

Works Cited   201

Bibliography   203

Index   207

About the Author   211

To the Instructor

The fifth edition of this book includes a number of noteworthy changes:

Chapter One, **Fundamentals of Thinking,** is expanded and reorganized to be both more informative and more useful to students. A new section discusses the relationship of intelligence to thinking and encourages students to take a more positive view of their intellectual potential. The sections on the principles of thinking and the fact/opinion discussion are revised and enlarged.

The treatment of persuasion, formerly in the final chapter of the book, is now in a new Chapter Two, **Persuasive Communication,** so that students can begin putting its strategies to use early in the course. The focus of the chapter is expanded to cover speaking and group discussion as well as writing. In addition, this chapter now provides help in overcoming the most serious errors in grammar and usage, which are not only lapses in "mechanics" but obstacles to persuasion.

The chapter entitled **Becoming an Individual** (formerly Chapter Two, now Chapter Three) is expanded. A new section, "Four Empowering Attitudes," describes the attitudes associated with success in college, career, and relationships. The treatment of manipulation is expanded and now includes an explanation of common devices used to manipulate others and strategies for avoiding those devices. A new section on "Habits for Individuality" is also added.

The chapter entitled **Evaluating Arguments** (now Chapter Four) is expanded to include a detailed treatment of the various kinds of evidence encountered in arguments; brief but comprehensive guides to conducting research in the library, on the Internet, and in personal interviews; a strategy for avoiding plagiarism; and a strategy for evaluating complex arguments

The chapter entitled **Applying Your Thinking Skills** (now Chapter Six) is expanded and invites the student to apply critical thinking to four new applications: *Everyday Problems, Relationships, Careers,* and *Ethical Judgments.* (Note: The treatment of problem solving, previously set off as a separate chapter, is now a unit within this chapter.)

"Good Thinking" units appear throughout the book. Each of these units offers a profile of an individual thinker (or a group of thinkers) worthy of respect and emulation. The intended effect is to inform students of the role of thinking in achievement and to offer models for students to emulate.

Introduction: Strategies for Effective Learning

How much you will benefit from this book, your other textbooks, and your overall educational experience will depend on your ability to learn. You may have heard that this ability can't be acquired; it is something you either have in your genes or you don't.

That view is wrong!

While it is true that some people learn more easily than others and seem to have an inborn talent that helps them be successful, there's another important factor that isn't found in people's genes—the strategies or "tricks" that enhance learning. Anyone can master these strategies and make learning easier and more enjoyable. In this section you'll learn a dozen simple yet powerful strategies.

▶ Good Thinking!

The Story of Frank and Lillian Gilbreth

This remarkable husband and wife team, both of whom were born in 1868, became pioneers in the science of time management. As a young apprentice, Frank studied master bricklayers and noted that they all used different motions. He also noted that each of their assistants had an individual way of placing the bricks and mortar; some did less bending, reaching, and lifting than others and were more efficient.

Gilbreth realized that having all the workers imitate the more efficient ones would result in a considerable cost saving, so he fitted each scaffold with a shelf for the bricks and mortar and had the bricks stacked conveniently. Ultimately his changes reduced the number of motions required to lay a brick from 18 to 4 and one-half. Gilbreth then became a building contractor and, later, a management engineer.

Eventually, Frank met and married Lillian, who had studied literature but then obtained a Ph.D. in industrial psychology. Both lectured at Purdue University and worked as management consultants, helping a wide variety of workers, including surgeons, save time, improve performance, and reduce fatigue. Their basic approach was to film workers at the jobs and then conduct exacting motion studies to determine optimum motion patterns.

Frank Gilbreth died in 1924. After his death, Lillian continued to use their approach to help injured individuals become productive despite their handicaps and to improve household efficiency. She died in 1972.

This amazing couple made all their contributions while raising twelve children. Their best-selling book, *Cheaper by the Dozen,* was made into a classic movie that is still shown from time to time on TV. A more recent version of their story starred Steve Martin.

For more information on the Gilbreths, see http://gilbrethnetwork.tripod.com/bio.html and/or http://access.tucson.org/~michael/hm_2.html.

Plan your days

Think of time as money and you'll be less likely to squander it.

Each morning (or the night before if you prefer) make a list of things to do and classify them according to importance: (1) tasks that *must* be completed today and (2) tasks to complete if time permits. The few minutes you spend doing this are a wise investment—they will help you keep focused and accomplish more.

As you plan, keep in mind the three axioms of efficiency:

ELIMINATE WHAT NEED NOT BE DONE

SIMPLIFY WHAT MUST BE DONE

COMBINE TASKS WHENEVER POSSIBLE

Refer to your list throughout the day to be sure you are still on track. If, as often happens, events of the day require you to revise your plan, try to maintain your priorities.

▶ Good Thinking!

The Story of Art Fry

Art Fry was a chemical engineer employed in the product development department of 3M Corporation. However, his best-known breakthrough idea didn't occur the workplace but in his church choir.

Fry enjoyed singing in his church's choir and, like members of choirs everywhere, was in the habit of marking the scheduled hymns with little pieces of paper. This way he would be able to turn to the appropriate hymn quickly and be ready to sing when the choirmaster gave the signal. Unfortunately, the little pieces of paper had a way of falling out, leaving him to hurriedly flip through the pages searching for the correct song.

Fry thought that there must be a way to get the slips of paper to stick to the page so that they wouldn't fall out, yet not tear the page when they were removed. He remembered a peculiar adhesive a fellow researcher had concocted a few years earlier. At that time no one had been able to think of a use for it.

Fry checked the files, got the formula, and made a batch of adhesive. It turned out to be too strong for his purposes. So he experimented with the formula and finally produced a glue that was like the little bear's porridge in the Goldilocks story—not too strong, not too weak, but just right. He took the idea to management and got approval to test-market the sample product, and the "Post-It" was born.

Fry's story illustrates the value of seeing frustration as an opportunity for achievement.

View frustrations as opportunities

Grumbling, griping, feeling defeated. These are common responses when things go wrong, and they are unfortunate. A much better response is summed up in the Japanese saying, "Bad news is good news!" Granted, such a response seems odd, if not downright loony. But the thinking behind it reveals wisdom: The realization that having something go wrong presents an opportunity, even an *invitation*, to set it right.

The habit of viewing frustration as opportunity has rewarded countless inventors and other creative people. Here are a few of their success stories:

- In 1853 24-year-old Levi Strauss traveled to San Francisco with bolts of heavy cloth from his brother's dry goods company in New York. He hoped miners would buy the material to use for their tents. Unfortunately, few miners were interested. But Strauss was not defeated by the experience. He tried to think of a more profitable use for the cloth. Realizing how hard the job of mining was on miners' clothes, he decided the heavy cloth would make sturdy work pants. Thus was born the famous product named after him—Levi jeans.

- On a hot summer day in 1904 Ole Evinrude and Bessie Cary went on a picnic to an island 2 and one-half miles from the shore of Lake Michigan. When they finished eating, she said she'd love to have a cold dish of ice cream for dessert. So Ole rowed to the mainland, got the ice cream, rowed back to the island and presented Bessie with . . . a dripping, runny mess. Why Ole didn't take Bessie with him to get the ice cream is not known. What is known is that his frustration over the experience led him to invent the first commercially successful outboard motor.

- In 1935 Paul Sperry took his cocker spaniel for a walk. The ground was covered with snow and ice, and Sperry had difficulty keeping his footing. But the dog had no such difficulty. Sperry turned his annoyance into curiosity and examined the pattern on the bottom of the dog's paws. Later he carved that pattern into a piece of crepe rubber and created the sole of what is today known as the boat shoe, which prevents slipping on wet decks.

- In 1948, after a walk in the woods, Swiss engineer George de Mestral found that cockleburs had stuck to his socks. Surely millions of people have had that same experience and merely cursed their misfortune. But de Mestral wondered what made them stick, so he put them under a microscope and saw hundreds of tiny hooks that grasped anything with loops, such as cloth. Putting that insight to work, de Mestral invented a method of duplicating nature's hooks and loops. The resulting product is known today as Velcro.

- One night in the 1950s Frank McNamara took some people to dinner and, when it was time to pay, realized he had no money with him. When he returned home, he vowed never to experience such embarrassment again . . . and proceeded to invent the credit card!

Whenever things go wrong for you, and you feel frustration, annoyance, or disappointment, remember these success stories and seize your opportunity.

Tackle unpleasant tasks immediately

When a task is unpleasant, do you tend to procrastinate? Most people do. You know you have to read that chapter, write that paper, or study for that test. You have every intention of doing so, but manage to find some excuse for not doing it just yet. Perhaps later today, you tell yourself, or better yet, *tomorrow*. As a result, it never gets done in a timely manner.

Procrastination prevents you from doing your best and adds tension to your life. It's hard to feel contented with yourself when you know that an unpleasant task awaits your attention. And the longer you wait, the larger it looms.

There is a simple solution to this situation. Put unpleasant tasks high on your list of priorities. Whenever possible, tackle them immediately. By doing so, you'll become a more dependable person. Equally important, you'll increase your sense of self-satisfaction.

Chip away at big jobs

Some tasks are just too big to accomplish at one time. For example, term papers and projects require you to spend considerable time in the library, conduct interviews with knowledgeable people on campus, outline your paper, and so on. You need a special strategy for getting such projects done on time.

The best approach is to break the project or paper into a number of parts, and spend a little time on it every few days. For example, each time you visit the library for another purpose, you might also consult one information source for your term paper. Similarly, after you have completed your research in small increments and created your outline, you can do the writing one small section at a time.

The advantage of this approach is that when due dates arrive and others are moaning, "I don't think I'll finish on time. Why, oh why didn't I start earlier?" you'll be calm and confident.

Take charge of your mind

Is your mind entirely under your control? Most people would answer yes, but many fail to realize just how often they operate on automatic pilot. Uninvited ideas drift in and out of their consciousness. Memories glitter and draw them back in time. Imagination creates pleasant little daydreams.

If you have experienced such mental meandering, you know how absorbing it can be. Minutes, even hours, seem to evaporate. Be honest—how many times have you sat in a classroom for almost an entire period, only to realize that while your body was present your mind was somewhere else entirely?

The human mind is prone to distraction, and mass culture has made the problem worse by shortening our attention spans. Television camera angles change every few seconds during programs and even more during commercials. This adds up to hundreds of forced attention shifts every hour we watch. Add to those the shifts we create ourselves by clicking the remote, and it's understandable that many people have trouble concentrating for even a few minutes.

How can you take charge of your mind? Become more aware of what it is doing from moment to moment. That way you'll know when you've lost concentration. When that happens, turn your attention back to what you were doing.

Will you ever reach a point where you will be able to concentrate automatically, without effort? No, nobody does. This is because concentrating, like steering a car, involves making constant slight adjustments. The process is necessary whether one has been driving for only a few weeks or for fifty years. Experience does make it easier, however.

Listen actively

Research has repeatedly shown that people retain, on average, less than half of what they hear. That's not good enough to succeed in college (or, for that matter, in most careers). The main reason for this retention problem is that the mind can process ideas at about 500 words a minute, whereas the average speaking rate is less than 150 words a minute. In other words, in the typical listening situation—such as a classroom lecture—the mind has too little to keep it occupied, so it wanders.

The solution is to change your mental state from passive to active, from merely waiting for information to actively processing information. The way to do this is simple—take notes. Don't try to get every word; you probably can't write fast enough for that. In some cases, you won't even be able to get every sentence. Direct your mind to identify the most important words and sentences (another task to keep it occupied) and record just those.

In addition to improving your listening, taking notes will also provide you with a valuable tool for exam preparation.

Refuse to tolerate confusion

If you don't understand something in class, do you raise your hand and ask for clarification? Many students don't. They would rather remain confused and risk getting a low grade than run the risk of appearing stupid. The risk is much smaller than they imagine. In many cases, it is nonexistent.

When one person doesn't understand something the chances are good that others don't understand it either. Have you ever approached fellow students after class and asked them a question, only to realize they were as confused as you? It happens all the time. When one student dares to ask for clarification, other students are likely to be grateful. And the instructor is likely to regard the one who asks as conscientious. Be that student!

Similarly, if you encounter a confusing passage while reading a textbook, don't just hope that the passing of time will clarify its meaning. Instead, reread the passage ALOUD and slowly, listening to the words. By adding hearing to seeing, you will often be able to break through the confusion.

Study efficiently

Would you believe that A and B students often spend less time studying than C and D students? It's true. The fact illustrates an important principle of learning—the amount of time spent studying is less important than the *circumstances.*

Here's how to get the most from your studying:

1. Choose the right **time.** If you are a "morning person" who jumps out of bed eager to meet the day's challenges, try to make that time of day your study time. On the other hand, if you are a "night owl" arrange your schedule accordingly.

2. Choose a suitable **place.** The best place is the one with the fewest distractions. You'll study more efficiently in a quiet corner of the library than in the campus snack bar. If there's not too much activity in and around the parking lot, consider studying in your car.

3. Choose favorable **conditions.** Don't confuse favorable with enjoyable. For example, you may enjoy having the TV blaring or having your Walkman playing, but, for learning, quiet beats noisy every time. (It should go without saying that even a little alcohol diminishes the effectiveness of studying.)

You may have to experiment a little to find what works best for you. But the payoff—faster, more efficient learning—is well worth the effort.

Capture insights

Insights are relatively rare and they arrive unexpectedly. What's more, they seldom pay us a return visit, so it's important to be ready to capture them when they come.

Keep a pencil and paper handy at all times. (If you prefer, carry a micro-tape recorder.) Whenever an interesting idea occurs to you—whether about a course you're taking, a relationship, or anything important to you—record it immediately.

Don't be shy about recording your ideas when you are in a group of people. In this day of pagers and cell phones, no one will think it odd if you say, "Excuse me, I've just thought of something important I don't want to forget."

Read for understanding

Reading is much more than running your eyes across the page and recognizing words. It involves grasping the *meaning* of what is written and understanding the relationship of each sentence and paragraph to all the others.

To get more from your reading, follow this approach:

1. Take about five minutes and **skim** the chapter or article. Pay particular attention to the first two paragraphs and the last paragraph; also pay attention to the headings.

2. Take another few minutes and **reflect** on what you found by skimming. Ask yourself: Is the author's main purpose to inform or to persuade the reader? What is the central idea of the piece? (This will usually be stated in the first or second paragraph and echoed in the last one.) What are the secondary ideas? (The headings should suggest them.)

3. Next, **read** the chapter or article. Keep a reasonable pace, neither rushing nor dawdling. Don't underline or highlight anything yet.

4. Finally, **review** what you have read. At this point, you should be clear about what is important and what is not. Mark the piece accordingly.

This approach will take you no more time than one laborious reading would. It may, in fact, take less. But it will increase your understanding of what you have read. (This approach is not only a good general one—it also has specific application in understanding complex arguments, as Chapter Four explains.)

Keep a journal

We rather quickly forget most of what we learn. This is especially true of what we learn from lectures and textbooks. Yet there is a way to increase the amount of material we retain—keep a journal of your learning experiences.

A journal doesn't require a great investment of time, just a little investment at appropriate times. One such time is immediately after each class and each study session. Here's what to do:

- Buy a middle-sized spiral or bound notebook to serve as your journal for the semester. Keep it with you whenever you attend class or study.

- If possible, when each class ends, instead of rushing out with the other students, stay in your seat for a few minutes, take out your notebook, and write down in a sentence or two the most important lesson you just learned. In some cases, the lesson will be something said during the instructor's lecture—for example, some clarifying explanation of a passage in the textbook. In other cases, it may be an insight that occurred to you while participating in class discussion, or one that another student expressed.

- Similarly, whenever you are approaching the end of a study session—for example, reading a chapter in the textbook—take a few minutes out to record in your journal, in your own words, the points that are too important to forget.

- From time to time, especially (but not only) before exams, read through your journal and refresh your recollection.

Turn these strategies into habits

Someone once observed that "approaching life without goals and strategies puts you at the mercy of events much as being in a canoe without a paddle puts you at the mercy of the current." This is a valuable insight, but here's an important footnote: To benefit from a paddle, you've got to put it into the water and pull. To benefit from the strategies for learning presented above, you've got to use them over and over until they become habitual.

Becoming a
Critical Thinker

Fundamentals of Thinking

IN THIS CHAPTER:

What is intelligence?
Intelligence is, most importantly, something you do.

What is thinking?
Thinking is a purposeful mental activity. You control it and not vice versa.

Key principles of thinking
These five reliable ideas provide the foundation for thinking.

Identifying facts and opinions
Facts are amply documented ideas. Opinions are open to dispute.

Checking facts and testing opinions
Facts can be misunderstood. Opinions can be mistaken. Both need to be tested.

Evaluating evidence
Evidence is information that supports an opinion but not all evidence is equally reliable.

Dare to change your mind
Changing your mind in response to evidence is a mark of courage and integrity.

A comprehensive thinking strategy
This four-step strategy will make your thinking consistently effective.

What is intelligence?

I n a scene from the movie *Forrest Gump,* Forrest was sitting on a bench next to an old man who asked him rudely, "Are you stupid?" Forrest gave the man his most dignified look and responded politely, "Stupid is as stupid does, sir." This wasn't just a clever comeback; it was and is a profound truth.

Intelligence isn't just something we *have.* It is, more importantly, something we *do.*

If this sounds strange to you, it could be because you've learned to associate intelligence only with *factual knowledge.* In this association, the human mind is little more than an information warehouse, the size of each person's warehouse is determined genetically and can't be expanded, and the most intelligent people are "walking encyclopedias" who can answer all the questions in class or win all the prizes on game shows.

Now there's nothing wrong with acquiring and storing information. It certainly beats ignorance. But the human mind has another, more exciting function—*using* information to solve problems, resolve issues,

and meet everyday challenges in living. From this perspective, the human mind is much more than an information warehouse. It is an idea factory, and the key to its success is a different kind of knowledge, *performance knowledge.*

Factual knowledge is *knowing about.* Performance knowledge is knowing how, sometimes referred to as "know-how." The terms are roughly equivalent, respectively, to "book smart" and "street smart." Both factual knowledge and performance contribute to intelligence, so it is unfortunate that they are thought to be in opposition to each other. But it is even more unfortunate that performance knowledge has been ignored since it is more active and dynamic. It also plays a greater role in our responses to everyday challenges. In that sense, it is the more practical measure of intelligence.

The main ingredient in performance knowledge is *thinking skill.* And here is the best news of all—whatever your present level of thinking skill, it can be raised. And as you raise it, you become more intelligent!

▶ Good Thinking!

The Story of Albert Einstein

Few people deserve the title "genius" more than Albert Einstein. His theory of relativity is one of the greatest intellectual achievements in human history.

Academically, however, Einstein was less than mediocre. One teacher told him he would "never amount to anything." Eventually, he was asked to leave school.

After spending some time traveling in Italy, Einstein applied to the Zurich Polytechnic School. He failed the admissions exam, and was required to return to high school for a year before being accepted. On graduating from Zurich he was rejected for an assistantship because no professor would give him a recommendation. He managed to get a job as a tutor but was soon fired.

Some years later, while working at odd jobs, Einstein submitted a doctoral thesis to the University of Zurich, but it was rejected. He eventually got a job in the patent office. In his spare time, he continued his studies, quietly earned a doctorate, and began publishing his scientific findings. Finally, after many years in relative obscurity, his work won him the recognition he deserved.

If Einstein had accepted his teachers' assessment of his intelligence, he would undoubtedly have lost the motivation to pursue his studies, and the world would be unimaginably poorer.

For more information on Albert Einstein, see www.nobel.se/physics/laureates/1921/einstein-bio.html.

What is thinking?

Imagine that you are staring into space, picturing yourself heading for the airport. You see yourself ready for a month's cruise in the Caribbean, your pockets stuffed with cash. Would this mental process be thinking?

Now imagine that you're discussing politics with friends. "It's always the same with politicians," you say. "They're full of promises until they're elected. Then they develop chronic amnesia." Would you be thinking in this case?

Thinking, as we will define it in this book, is a purposeful mental activity. You control it, not vice versa. For the most part, thinking is a conscious activity. Yet the unconscious mind can continue working on a problem after conscious activity stops—for example, while you sleep.

Given this definition, your ruminations about a Caribbean cruise are not thinking but daydreaming; you are merely following the drift of your fantasies. On the other hand, your discussion of politics could constitute thinking, as long as you aren't just repeating something you've said or heard before.

Thinking is sometimes regarded as two harmonious processes. One process is the production of ideas (creative thinking), accomplished by *widening* your focus and looking at many possibilities. The other process is the evaluation of ideas (critical thinking), accomplished by narrowing your focus, sorting out the ideas you've generated, and identifying the almost reasonable ones. Both processes can be improved by training and practice.

Our discussion in this chapter and throughout the book will include some approaches for producing ideas, but its main focus will be evaluating ideas—that is, critical thinking. Chances are you received little or no critical thinking instruction in high school. Your teachers were not to blame for this. In many cases they, and their teachers before them, were denied such training, largely because of the theory that thinking can't be taught or that some subjects teach it automatically. Such erroneous ideas resisted correction for most of the twentieth century.

Thinking can be taught, and not just to "gifted" students but to all students. No course automatically teaches thinking, though any course can teach it when teachers make thinking skills a direct objective and give students regular practice in producing and evaluating ideas.[1] Such instruction

---

[1] In *An Experiment in the Development of Critical Thinking,* Edward Glaser cited more than 340 studies. In subsequent decades hundreds more studies on critical and creative thinking were published. Notable among the researchers on creative thinking are Sidney Parnes, J. P. Guilford, and E. Paul Torrance. More recent researchers on thinking and intelligence include Howard Gardner, Robert Sternberg, and David Perkins.

benefits students in their studies, their careers, community service, and personal relationships. According to psychologist Albert Ellis, "[People] can live the most self-fulfilling, creative, and emotionally satisfying life by intelligently organizing and disciplining [their] thinking."

Unfortunately, shallow, illogical thinking is common. For example, a drug or alcohol abuser may tell himself, "I'm not addicted—I can quit any time I want." A painfully thin anorexic may persuade herself that she is grossly overweight. Even highly educated people may reason that they can never contract a sexually transmitted disease if they have sex only with "nice" people." Abusive parents may think that screaming and hitting are appropriate ways of disciplining children.

There are even worse examples of poor thinking. A woman doused her husband with rubbing alcohol and set him on fire because he had been acting crazy and refusing to work. She reasoned that by setting him on fire she'd get him into the hospital for some help. A father kept his 18-year-old daughter chained in the basement because he was afraid she would become a prostitute. An elderly woman robbed a bank, then jumped on her *three-wheel bike* and pedaled away. (Police caught her a couple of blocks from the scene.)

Thinking errors as extreme as these are easy to recognize. Others are more difficult, especially when they are our own rather than other people's ideas. And the most difficult to discern are those enshrined in popular culture. It's easy to assume that other people have examined such ideas and found them worthy, when that may not be the case. For this reason, we should question most vigorously the ideas we are tempted to take for granted—familiar, fashionable ideas.

Key principles of thinking

Thinking is like building a house or a skyscraper—the success of the enterprise depends on the firmness of the foundation. The foundation of thinking, of course, is not concrete and steel but *principles*—ideas that have survived rigorous testing and proved trustworthy. The following principles of thinking are among the most important:

Truth is discovered, not created

You have probably heard it said that truth is subjective and personal, or that each person creates truth to his or her own specifications. This belief is common today, and it means that believing something is so *actually makes it so.* In other words, reality is whatever we wish it to be.

This idea directly contradicts the view that has been generally accepted since ancient times—the view that *truth is the accurate representation of objective reality.* In this view reality is unaffected by our wishes, preferences, and assumptions.

Is the new view that truth is created and subjective more reasonable than the traditional view that truth is objective? Perhaps the best way to tell is to consider what the new view of truth implies about everyday issues. ***If truth is created by each person, then . . .***

. . . Galileo's assertion that the sun is the center of the solar system, a view that shocked most people of his time, is not true for everyone but just for those who want to believe it.

. . . those who believe that the earth is flat, the Holocaust never happened, and Saddam Hussein was a benevolent leader of his people are correct. And so are those who take opposite views.

. . . when a drunk falls into an empty swimming pool thinking that it is full, water will suddenly appear and save him from a hard landing.

. . . the standard courtroom oath—"I swear to tell the truth, the whole truth, and nothing but the truth"—is outdated. Witnesses should be allowed to testify to their own personal truth and no one's truth should be considered superior to anyone else's. Moreover, since defendants' pleas of not guilty are equal to prosecutors' claims of guilt, all court cases should be dismissed.

. . . it is a waste of time for archeologists to dig for proof of lost civilizations, for medical researchers to search for the causes and cures of diseases, for historians to pore over dusty manuscripts for clues to the past, and for students to read textbooks like this one. Instead, they should simply decide what they want to believe and—presto!—it will become reality.

. . . all your incorrect answers on past true/false tests should be marked correct and your grade-point average raised accordingly.

As even these few examples make clear, the notion that truth is created by each individual does not hold up under scrutiny. In contrast, everyday experience confirms the principle that truth is discovered.

▚ Exercise 1

Throughout this century, a famous painting entitled The Man with the Golden Helmet was believed to be the work of the Dutch master Rembrandt. Some years ago it was proved to have been painted by someone else. Some people would say that the truth about this painting changed. Do you agree? Explain.

_____

_____

_____

⤴ Exercise 2

Examine each of the following cases in light of what you've learned about truth in this section. State your view and explain why you hold it.

Ira is a journalist. Will the belief that he can create his own truth make him more or less likely to value accuracy in his reporting?

_____

_____

_____

Bruce is prejudiced toward minorities and women. Which of the following beliefs would be more helpful in overcoming his prejudice: the belief that truth is subjective and created; or the belief that truth is objective and discovered? Explain your reasoning.

_____

_____

_____

Most students can use additional motivation to learn. Will the belief that they can create their own truth help or hinder their motivation? Explain.

_____

_____

_____

A statement can't be both true and false at the same time and in the same way

This principle is known as the principle of contradiction. The following examples demonstrate the validity of this principle:

Statement: My roommate borrowed my sweater without permission. *Comment:* If this statement were both true and false at the same time in the same way, it would mean that you simultaneously *gave* your permission and *didn't give* your permission. That is impossible. You must either have given your approval or not given it. This example confirms the principle of contradiction.

Statement: During World War II the Nazis killed millions of Jews in concentration camps. *Comment:* Either the Nazis did this horrible deed or they didn't. Since there is no way they did it and didn't do it, this example also supports the principle of contradiction.

Statement: Capital punishment is a deterrent to crime. *Comment:* Let's assume for the sake of discussion that capital punishment was once a deterrent to crime but no longer is. In other words, that this statement was true at one time but is false today. Does this situation challenge the principle of contradiction? No. The principle specifies that a statement cannot be both true and false *at the same time* in the same way.

Statement: Edgar is richer than Clem. *Comment:* If Edgar has more money than Clem, but Clem surpasses him in moral character, then the statement would be both true and false but not *in the same way*. It would be true in one sense and false in another. (To be a contradiction, it would have to say Edgar has more money than Clem *and* does not have more money than Clem.) Thus, this example also confirms the principle of contradiction.

A note of caution: The principle of contradiction applies whenever opposing statements make *exactly opposite* assertions—for example, *she is* versus *she isn't, he did* versus *he didn't, they have* versus *they haven't*. In such cases, it is certain that one statement must be true and the other false. However, when the assertions made are not exactly opposite but merely different, both could be false. For example, if you say "Sally got the highest mark on the exam" and I say "Luke got the highest mark," it is possible that we are both mistaken. (Bertha or Juwan may have gotten the highest mark.)

Exercise 3

Classify each of the following exchanges as (a) an actual contradiction or (b) a near contradiction. Briefly explain each choice.

Mavis: *Big time college sports are corrupt.*
Cora: *You're absolutely wrong, Mavis.*

_____

_____

_____

Karen: *There are very few real heroes today.*
Hanna: *I think there are more today than there have ever been.*

_____

_____

_____

⏩ Exercise 3 (cont.)

Brad: *Look at that new Lincoln across the street.*
Clara: *That isn't a Lincoln—it's a Mercury.*

_____

_____

_____

All people make mistakes, even experts

It's a shame that there are no official accuracy statistics available for experts in the various fields of knowledge. If there were, you could check the experts' "batting averages." You might be shocked to learn just how often experts are wrong. Bennett Cerf and Victor Navasky have written an interesting collection of wrong judgments and predictions made by experts. (Cerf) Many are so far off the mark that they are laughable. Here is a brief sampling:

- A British scientist in 1895: "Heavier-than-air flying machines are impossible."
- A London professor at the dawn of the railroad, when the top speed was 25 mph: "Rail travel at high speed is not possible because passengers, unable to breathe, would die of asphyxia."
- The commissioner of the U.S. Office of Patents, arguing for the abolition of his office in 1899: "Everything that can be invented has been invented."
- The President of the British Royal Society in 1900: "X-rays are a hoax."
- A banker, in 1903, advising against investing in Ford Motor Co: "The horse is here to stay, but the automobile is only a novelty—a fad."
- A famous movie studio head, commenting on the future of TV: "People will soon get tired of staring at a plywood box every night."
- *Variety* magazine's assessment of rock and roll in 1955: "It will be gone by June."
- An editor, in 1957, turning down a book on computers: "[I have it] on the highest authority that data processing is a fad and won't last out the year."

This is not to say that the "batting averages" of experts are lower than those of non-experts. As a rule, they are considerably higher. The most sensible approach is therefore not to settle for a single expert's opinion but to seek a second, and perhaps a third, expert opinion before making up your mind. In addition, since advanced degrees are not awarded with crystal balls, be especially wary when any expert attempts to predict the future.

▶ Good Thinking!

The Story of Elizabeth Loftus

The majority of men and women engaged in scholarly research don't get invited to the talk shows or have stories written about them in popular magazines, even when their work has a significant effect on people's lives. Psychologist Elizabeth Loftus is an exception. One reason is that her research has challenged some long-standing beliefs about human memory. Another is the relevance of that research to some prominent controversies of the last decade or two.

The traditional view is that memory is like a videotaped record of events etched into the grooves of our minds. According to this theory, a particular record may become hidden, even from ourselves, but it is never lost. Given our desire and, in some cases, the assistance of people experienced in recovering such "data," we can recover any memory, however traumatic. And what we recover will be accurate to the smallest detail.

A number of researchers have challenged this traditional view of memory, but none as effectively as Loftus. She devised her own research projects and proved that real memories can be altered, and that fictitious memories can be created. In experiments with children and adults she first showed them short films and later discussed their recollections of what they saw. In one experiment, by merely asking "Did you see a bear?" or "Did you see a boat?" she was able to make them remember details that were not present in the film.

In another case, by using the word "smash" instead of "hit" she was able to change people's estimate of the speed of cars AND to create a memory of broken glass where there had been none.

For more information on Elizabeth Loftus, see Elizabeth Loftus and Katherine Ketcham, *Witness for the Defense* (New York: St. Martin's Press, 1991) or Elizabeth Loftus, *Eyewitness Testimony* (Cambridge, MA: Harvard University Press, 1996).

Ideas can be examined without being embraced

Some people refuse to consider an idea that differs from their own out of loyalty to their convictions. This refusal is especially strong in political and religious matters.

For example, a conservative might refuse to read an article by a liberal and a Christian might refuse to listen to a lecture on Judaism, Buddhism, or Islam. Such people prevent themselves from deepening their understanding. Also, because knowledge is as essential to thinking as air is to breathing, they stifle their intellectual development and do themselves a disservice.

Whenever you are tempted to deny a fair hearing to unfamiliar or opposing ideas, remind yourself that examining an idea is not the same as embracing it. If, after applying critical thinking, you decide that an idea is unworthy, you will have a substantial basis for rejecting it. Moreover, you will be in a better position to explain its flaws to others.

Feeling is no substitute for thinking

Following feelings, impulses, and impressions is fashionable today. Some people go so far as to say that feelings are a *better* guide than thoughts. This is a comforting idea, but in order to believe it you have to overlook the many times when feelings led you astray.

Consider a time when you were trying to lose weight and your feelings said, "Order the double hot fudge sundae." Or another time when you felt the urge to tell your instructor or the boss what you *really* thought of her. Or occasions when you felt the impulse to go to a party instead of studying for a test, charge an expensive item you didn't need and couldn't afford, or drive 30 miles an hour over the speed limit to avoid being late. No doubt you can think of many additional examples of feelings that, if followed, would have caused you pain or misfortune.

Louis L'Amour, vagabond and author of dozens of western novels, tells a story from his days as a laborer in an Oregon lumber mill. The story illustrates the danger of relying on feelings, impulses, and impressions:

> They put a number of us to digging holes four feet square and down to hardpan for concrete piers to support a building soon to be erected. There were at least a dozen of us on the job and the ground was partly frozen. After we got down a short distance, water had to be bailed out, so progress was slow. There was a husky young German, a couple of years older than I, and we got into a contest to make the work more fun. The average was two and a half holes per

day, while several were doing three. The German and I were doing four holes apiece.

Our boss was an easygoing Irishman who saw what was going on and wisely stayed out of it, but the management in its wisdom decided he was not gung-ho enough as a boss and brought in a new man.

Knowing nothing of any of us, he came suddenly into the area and found the German and me leaning on our shovels, having just finished our second holes for the day, while nobody else had finished one. He promptly fired both of us for loafing along with another chap who had been doing three holes a day. In his first day on the job he had fired his three best men (L'Amour, 105).

The problem with following feelings, urges, and impressions is not that they always lead us astray. (They don't.) The problem is that they aren't consistently reliable. Sometimes they advise us well and sometimes they don't. In L'Amour's example, the new boss's mistake was to act on his immediate impression instead of examining it critically.

Rather than mindlessly following your feelings, think about them carefully and decide whether they *deserve* to be followed.

Identifying facts and opinions

One of the most basic activities in critical thinking is distinguishing facts from opinions. Facts are ideas whose accuracy is clearly and amply documented and affirmed by knowledgeable people. Opinions are ideas that have not yet been sufficiently documented and are therefore still open to dispute.

Despite the clarity and simplicity of these definitions, the task of distinguishing facts from opinions can be difficult. One reason is that not every *statement* of fact is factual. The most obvious example is a lie—for example, a child saying she didn't eat the cookies when she did or the perpetrator of a crime swearing he is innocent. In addition to lies, there are honest mistakes. A person might misread a memo and tell a colleague a meeting is scheduled for three o'clock today when it is actually scheduled for tomorrow. Or an art expert might declare a painting to be the work of a master and only later discover it is a brilliant forgery. For years it was considered a fact that the earth is flat. (Believe or not, there is still a Flat Earth Society composed of people who cling to the discredited "fact.")

Another reason that facts and opinions can be difficult to distinguish is that opinions are often stated *as if* they were facts. Consider these statements: "The death penalty constitutes cruel and unusual punishment"; "The cause of children committing crimes is irresponsible parenting." Each statement appears to be factual because of the way it is stated. Yet informed people continue to disagree about each. Therefore each statement is an opinion. (This is not to say that either of these statements is false, only that neither issue has been settled.)

Over time some opinions acquire the status of facts. For example, in the nineteenth century it was standard practice for physicians to handle cadavers in the hospital morgue and then, without washing their hands, make their rounds and visit patients. When one perceptive physician, Ignaz Semmelweiss, expressed the opinion that this practice might be responsible for spreading infections, he was ridiculed and ostracized. Today his "absurd" opinion is universally recognized as a fact.

The following examples illustrate the challenge of separating facts from opinions.

Statement: The 2000 Summer Olympic Games were held in Tokyo. *Comment:* This statement has the form of a fact, yet it is not factual. The 2000 Summer Olympic Games were held in Sydney, Australia.

Statement: Camel's hair brushes are made of Siberian squirrel fur. *Comment:* The statement appears ridiculous, yet it is factual.

Statement: Stalin was more brutal than Hitler. *Comment:* This statement is an opinion, but it is so well supported by historical evidence that many would consider it a fact.

Statement: Eyewitness testimony is generally unreliable. *Comment:* Anyone unfamiliar with the relevant research would consider this an opinion, and a wrong one at that. Yet it is a fact.

The following simple guidelines will help you decide whether any statement is a fact or an opinion:

1. **If a statement is common knowledge, it is a fact and need not be supported.**
   Example: Both John and Robert Kennedy were assassinated.
   Example: The cost of a college education is significantly higher today than it was twenty years ago.
   Comment: Both statements are common knowledge, so no support is needed.

2. **If a statement is not common knowledge yet has been confirmed to be accurate, it is a fact and need not be supported. However, the source of the confirmation should be cited.**

Example: The gray reef shark uses unusual body language to signal that it feels threatened.

Comment: This fact is not well known, at least among laypeople, so the source should be cited. (It is Bill Curtsinger, "Close Encounters with the Gray Reef Shark," *National Geographic*, January, 1995, 45–67.)

3. **If the statement is neither common knowledge nor confirmed to be accurate, it is an opinion and should be supported with evidence—that is, with reliable information.**

Example: More Americans are victimized by chronic laziness than by workaholism.

Comment: Some people will disagree, and others may ask, "Why does the author think this? What reasons does he or she have for holding this view rather than some competing view?" The person making the statement should provide answers to such questions.

4. **If it is not clear whether a statement is a fact or an opinion, treat it as an opinion.**

Remember another important point about opinion. As used in critical thinking, the term *opinion* refers only to matters of judgment, not to matters of taste or personal preference. The ancient Romans used to say that there is no way to argue profitably or think critically about matters of taste. Their view is as wise today as it was a couple of millennia ago.

Do you favor a slender figure or a full figure? Do you find long or short hair more appealing? Do you prefer fitted jeans or ones with the crotch down around the knees? Do you regard the Lincoln Town Car as beautiful or ugly? Do you enjoy sitcoms more than soap operas? All of these are matters of personal preference or taste **which cannot be supported by facts.**

As long as you express matters of taste *as matters of taste* you need not defend them, even if others find your tastes odd. Thus you should say "I prefer long hair" rather than "Long hair is more attractive than short hair," "I prefer the look of the Lincoln Town Car" rather than "The Lincoln Town Car is the most stylish car on the road," and "I enjoy sitcoms more than soap operas" rather than "Sitcoms are superior entertainment."

▶ Exercise 4

On a separate sheet of paper, indicate whether each of the following statements is
  a. clearly a fact.
  b. possibly a fact, but not clear without documentation.

▰ Exercise 4 (cont.)

c. an opinion.

d. a personal preference expressed as a personal preference.

e. a personal preference incorrectly expressed as an opinion.

Remember that it is sometimes difficult to separate facts and opinions. There may be room for disagreement over some answers, so be prepared to explain your choices.

1. I find blue-eyed redheads appealing.
2. The Chevrolet Camaro is the most stylish car on the market.
3. All religions share the same fundamental truths.
4. Darwin's theory of evolution continues to be controversial.
5. Pornography is an insult to women.
6. Black people are the victims of crime more often than white people.
7. Prostitution should be legalized.
8. People who need organ transplants greatly outnumber organ donors.
9. The publicity given to suicides leads to most "copycat" suicide attempts.
10. Comic books are as instructive about life as novels are.
11. Most students who drop out of school lack the intelligence to succeed.
12. Surgical procedures have been performed on fetuses while they were still in the uterus.

▰ Exercise 5

Now take the statements in the previous exercise and do as follows:

- For each that you classified b, state one or more reliable sources that could be cited to support the statement (assuming that the statement is factual).
- For each that you classified as b, possibly a fact, write questions that might be raised about the statement.
- If you classified any statement e, rewrite it as a personal preference rather than as an opinion.

Checking facts and testing opinions

We have already noted one reason for checking the facts about an issue—people sometimes misstate them. But there is another, equally good reason. People sometimes omit important facts. It doesn't matter whether the misstatement or omission is accidental or on purpose. Either way, if we fail to check, our evaluation may be flawed.

Often you will be able to check the facts of an issue by consulting an appropriate reference book, such as an encyclopedia, an almanac, a newspaper archive, or a dictionary. At other times, you will have to consult the research literature in the field. Chapter Four, "Evaluating Arguments," includes detailed advice on doing library and Internet research. You may wish to skim those sections now and refer to them whenever you are doing an exercise that calls for research.

The idea of testing opinions may seem odder than checking facts because it has become fashionable to think of opinions as something sacred and above criticism. Many people reason, "I have a right to my opinion—therefore my opinion must be right." They would be shocked to learn that for centuries before our time, opinion was not so highly regarded.

Almost 2,000 years ago the Greek philosopher Epictetus wrote: "Here is the beginning of philosophy: a recognition of the conflicts between men, a search for their cause, *a condemnation of mere opinion* . . . and the discovery of a standard of judgment." [Emphasis added.] Nineteenth-century British author Sir Robert Peel termed public opinion "a compound of folly, weakness, prejudice, wrong feeling, right feeling, obstinacy, and newspaper paragraphs."

American author John Erskine sarcastically termed opinion "that exercise of the human will which helps us to make a decision without information." American philosopher George Santayana observed that "people are usually more firmly convinced that their opinions are precious than that they are true." And one humorist suggested that many opinions that are expressed ought to have been sent by *slow freight* instead.

If you reflect on these skeptical views of opinion, you will appreciate that they underline an important reality—not all opinions are equally sound. Some are wise, others are foolish, and most fall somewhere between the two extremes. Unfortunately, most of us tend to forget this when forming opinions. Armed with little more than a sketchy news report, an assertion by a celebrity, or a fleeting impression, we may form opinions on complex subjects, such as the causes of child abuse, the reason why dinosaurs became extinct, or the health benefits of the latest diet.

Some time ago, a roving reporter took his tape recorder into the street and asked passersby, "How serious is racial tension in New York?" Among those who responded were a porter, two teachers, a truck driver, a film editor, a security guard, and a secretary. Chances are that at least some of these people lacked sufficient knowledge to form an opinion, but that didn't stop them from expressing one. (Perhaps they never heard the old saying, "It's better to remain silent and be thought a fool than to express your thoughts and remove all doubt.")

To be a critical thinker, you will need to develop the habit of testing opinions—your own as well as other people's—before trusting them. Here are seven effective ways of doing so.

Consult everyday experience

Consider your personal experience as well as what you know to be the experience of other people. If the opinion in question challenges that experience, it is almost certainly mistaken, at least in part. For example, Wayne Dyer, a popular author of self-help books says that guilt is "not a natural behavior" and "useless," and that it should be "exterminated" (Dyer, 90–91). Yet experience suggests that most people—particularly kind and considerate ones—feel guilt when they offend others. It's precisely their guilty feelings that motivate them to apologize for their bad behavior and to make amends. Dyer's idea is, at best, an overstatement.

Consider the opinion's likely consequences

One way to recognize that an opinion is flawed is if it leads to un-intended—and sometimes *undesired*—consequences. Not long ago zeal-ous advocates of African American studies courses expressed the opinion that only African Americans should be allowed to teach such courses. But then Arthur Schlesinger Jr., a well-known historian, pointed out that such a prohibition would have unintended consequences. He wrote: "The doctrine that only blacks can teach and write black history leads inexorably to the doctrine that blacks can teach and write only black history as well as to inescapable corollaries: Chinese must be restricted to Chinese history, women to women's history, and so on" (Schlesinger, 105).

Suppose you were evaluating this opinion: "The welfare system that continues to drain our tax dollars should not be gradually phased out but ended immediately." Among the consequences you would identify would be (1) some able-bodied welfare recipients would seek work and find it; (2) others would be less successful in their search; (3) those who are too old or too ill to work would be left with no source of income; (4) the living conditions for some children on welfare would decline; and (5) private agencies such as the Salvation Army would increase their giving. After examining these consequences, you would no doubt con-clude that the opinion, as stated, is unreasonable.

Consider the implications

This approach entails identifying and examining related ideas suggest-ed by the opinion. Let's say the opinion is, "What people view in movies or on television has no effect on their behavior." (Media spokespeople often say this in response to complaints that graphic sex and violence have a negative social impact.)

The implications of this conclusion are that viewing films and tele-vision programs can not degrade, inspire, or motivate us. If this were really the case, then public service announcements to drive sober and practice safe sex would be pointless and advertisers would be wasting millions of dollars on them.

Think of exceptions

This approach is useful when you are evaluating an opinion that expresses a general rule. The more exceptions you can think of, the more suspect the opinion is. Carl Rogers, a famous psychologist, wrote: "One of the basic things which I was a long time in realizing, and which I am still learning, is that when an activity feels as though it is valuable or worth doing, it is worth doing"(Rogers, 22). To test this idea think of activities that someone might feel are worth doing but really aren't. Here are just a few: shoplifting, lying on a résumé, expressing to an instructor your negative assessment of his teaching ability.

Here is another example of thinking of exceptions. A commonly expressed opinion is, "If you are strongly motivated, you can be anything you want to be." A notable exception is Michael Jordan's attempt to be a major league baseball player. He certainly did not lack motivation, and his basketball career proved he was a gifted athlete. Despite these advantages, however, he was unable to succeed in baseball. Jordan's case raises questions about the soundness of the opinion.

Think of counterexamples

Suppose an author is arguing that parents should not give children responsibilities until they are in their teens, and supports her argument with a number of case histories like this one: "I know a person who was given responsibilities such as picking up his clothes and toys at age 3; taking out the garbage at age 6; and raking leaves, washing dishes, and doing laundry at age 10. Today he's in his mid-thirties and resents having had all those chores." A counterexample would be the case of someone (perhaps you) who had similar responsibilities in childhood and now regards the experience as valuable. The more counterexamples you identify, the more justified you are in wondering about the reasonableness of the author's opinion.

Scholars in every field use the technique of finding counterexamples. Some time ago the issue of repressed memory was in the news. People undergoing therapy suddenly recalled horrible incidents of physical or sexual abuse they had supposedly suffered as children. Some therapists said they were suffering from "traumatic amnesia" and that victims of multiple instances of abuse were more likely to suffer from it than were victims of a single instance. This opinion sounded logical. But at least one critical thinker offered some powerful counterexamples—slaves, survivors of concentration camps in World War II, and victims of torture and political persecution. She noted that all these people suffered intense abuse for years yet never for a moment forgot it. (Hagen, 39) These counterexamples did not disprove the idea that memories of abuse can be repressed, but they did suggest the possibility that some claims of repressed memories, though perhaps sincere, are nevertheless false.

Reverse the opinion

This test consists of taking the exact opposite of the opinion you are examining and determining if a case can be made for it. Consider the popular opinion that "people must feel good about themselves before they are able to achieve." The reverse of that idea would be "people must achieve before they can feel good about themselves." A little investigation will reveal that this is not a new belief but the one that prevailed for hundreds, even thousands, of years before the self-esteem movement became dominant. To decide which of the two opinions is more reasonable, you might consider ordinary achievements in your own life—such as learning how to tie your shoes, whistle, ride a bike, dribble a basketball, drive a car, surf, or use a computer—and then decide whether self-esteem preceded or followed the achievement.

Look for relevant research

Every subject from agriculture to zoology has its devoted students, individuals who have spent decades learning everything they can about it and sharing their knowledge with others. These individuals are as near as the library or the Internet. One of the best ways to test any opinion is to see what these knowledgeable people have to say about it. (Chapter Four explains how to conduct research. Feel free to look ahead and read that explanation now.)

▨ Exercise 6

This exercise will give you an opportunity to apply the above techniques. Evaluate these opinions using one or more of the approaches explained above. If you wish, do this work on a separate sheet of paper.

A famous movie actress explained her decision to nurse her child until she was 2 years old: "That's a particular philosophy I have . . . allowing her to make her own decisions. I feel she is a better judge than I am."

_____

_____

_____

_____

_____

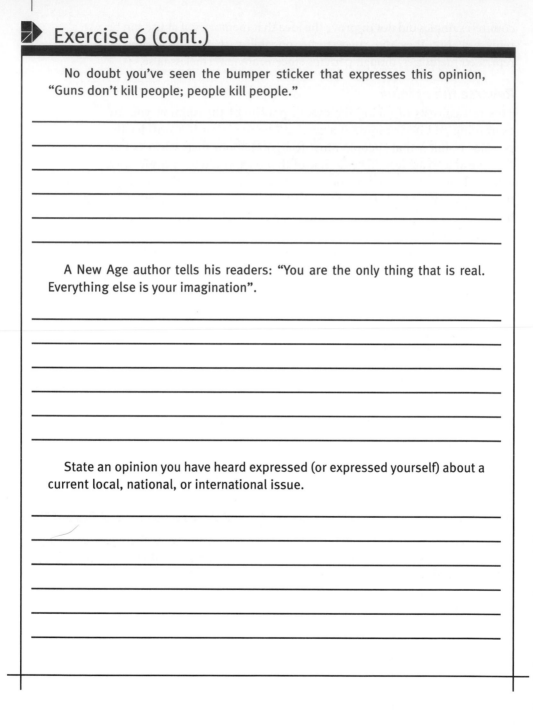

Exercise 6 (cont.)

No doubt you've seen the bumper sticker that expresses this opinion, "Guns don't kill people; people kill people."

_____

_____

_____

_____

_____

_____

A New Age author tells his readers: "You are the only thing that is real. Everything else is your imagination".

_____

_____

_____

_____

_____

_____

State an opinion you have heard expressed (or expressed yourself) about a current local, national, or international issue.

_____

_____

_____

_____

_____

_____

Evaluating evidence

As we have noted, evidence is reliable information that supports an opinion. The most common kind of evidence, the kind we will discuss here, is *reasons*. (Other kinds of evidence are discussed in Chapter Four.) A reason is the basis for thinking or doing something and is commonly signaled by the word "because." A child may say, "I hit Tommy because he made a face at me." A parent may say, "I sent my child to a private tutor because she was doing poorly in English." A prospective car buyer may explain, "I am considering a hybrid model because I do a lot of traveling and need an economical vehicle." In some cases, the word "because" is implied rather than stated. For example, Tawana may say, "I will never confide in Maria again. I once shared a secret with her and she blabbed it all over campus." Or a voter may say, "I certainly will not vote for that candidate for president. I don't like his mustache."

A moment's reflection on these few examples will reveal that some reasons are good and others aren't. Poor grades in English are a good reason for seeking a tutor, improved gas economy is a good reason for buying a car, and past betrayals are a good reason for not trusting someone. On the other hand, the fact that someone "made a face" is not a good reason for hitting him, and disliking a mustache is not a good reason to reject a candidate. (Incidentally, the mustache example is not as far-fetched as it sounds. Some historians regard it as a factor in Thomas Dewey's loss of the presidency to Harry Truman in 1948.)

In some cases a reason will be good but not *sufficient* to support the thought or action. Suppose that an executive position is open in a company and Martha and Bill are in contention for it. One member of the group who will make the decision says, "I am in favor of giving the position to Martha rather than to Bill because our company doesn't have enough women in upper management." The reason for promoting Martha—increasing the number of women in upper management—is certainly good. However, it would be *sufficient* only if Martha's qualifications were equal or superior to Bill's.

Here are some additional examples, together with comments to demonstrate how to evaluate reasons:

Example: "That exam wasn't fair because it tested us on material that we were specifically told we weren't responsible for."
Comment: The reason, if accurate, is both good and sufficient. Teachers have an obligation to keep their word.

Example: "That story about Britney Spears is probably false. After it appeared in a supermarket tabloid, no other newspaper or broadcast agency reported it." *Comment:* The reason for suspecting that the story is false is both good and sufficient. Supermarket tabloids have a reputation for exaggeration and misstatement. It is therefore reasonable to be suspicious about their stories, particularly when other news sources do not confirm them.

Example: "Management acted properly in installing surveillance cameras in the employee lounge and restrooms because they have a right to identify troublemakers in the firm." *Comment:* The reason offered—management's right to identify troublemakers—might justify installing surveillance cameras in work areas, but not in areas in which employees have the right of privacy. So the reason is neither good nor sufficient.

Example: "Taking money from my employer's petty cash fund isn't really stealing. My employer pays me less money than the person I replaced. He has also given me more responsibilities. And if I didn't take that money, I wouldn't be able to pay my bills." *Comment:* The reasons offered would support looking for another job but not stealing from the employer. As used here, the reasons are an attempt to justify behavior that is both unethical and criminal.

It is challenging enough to evaluate reasons when they are stated directly, but the challenge is even greater when they are left unstated. Unfortunately, the latter happens fairly often. The person may regard the opinion or action as self-supporting or may believe there is no need to justify it to other people. In addition, people sometimes *hide* the real reasons for their behavior, even from themselves. For example, a teenager may persuade himself that he smokes cigarettes because he enjoys doing so when the real reason is fear that his peers will laugh at him if he doesn't smoke.

Exercise 7

In each of the following cases, decide whether the reason offered is both good and sufficient to support the opinion or action.

Your Honor, I believe I was justified in hitting my wife. She kept nagging me about getting a job.

I didn't sign that petition. The person who asked me to sign refused to support my proposal last year.

I oppose government funding for abortions. It requires taxpayers to finance a procedure that many of them believe is a moral outrage.

Students who are caught cheating should receive a failing grade in the course. Cheating is a serious violation of scholarly integrity.

Women should not take their husbands' names when they marry. Doing so is a sign of subjugation.

Dare to change your mind

Some people believe that changing one's mind signals a lack of conviction. This belief allows them to think critically about other people's ideas but not about their own ideas. To maintain this double standard, they are forced to ignore unpleasant facts, defend unworthy views, and value ego more highly than truth.

▶ Good Thinking!

The Story of Stanton Samenow

Stanton Samenow's first job as a clinical psychologist was working with young criminals in a hospital psychiatric unit. He brought to the job a conviction that criminals were victims of early traumatic experiences, poverty, and family instability. His treatment was based on that viewpoint. The only problem was, the treatment didn't work.

Eventually a family friend, Dr. Samuel Yochelson, issued Samenow an invitation and a promise: If Samenow would join Yochelson in the latter's work with criminals, he would learn a new and much more successful treatment theory and approach. Samenow accepted the invitation and, in time, realized the promise.

Samenow discovered that his assumptions about criminals had been seriously mistaken. He learned, in his words, "that criminals choose to commit crimes. Crime resides within the person and is 'caused' by the way he thinks, not by his environment. Criminals think differently from responsible people. What must change is how the offender views himself and the world. Focusing on forces outside the criminal is futile."

The approach consisted of having criminals keep meticulous journals, in which they wrote down the thoughts they entertained day to day. Then they met in small groups and learned ways to change their thinking patterns. Stanton himself has worked with many hundreds of criminals, Yochelson with many more, and their success rate has been impressive. Samenow details his experiences with the program in his book *Inside the Criminal Mind*.

The obvious lesson in Samenow's story concerns his discoveries that the problem of crime is that "we are as we think" and that people who are in the habit of thinking irresponsible, harmful thoughts can change that habit. But there is another broader lesson in his story, one that reflects Samenow's own behavior. When his original theory proved mistaken, he set it aside, re-thought the matter, and developed a more reasonable theory. In short, he dared to change his mind.

For more information on Stanton Samenow see Stanton Samenow, *Inside the Criminal Mind* (New York: Times Books, 1984).

It is easy to identify people who harbor this belief. They treat all their opinions as if they were convictions and all their convictions as unquestionable. They are quick to disagree with views that differ from theirs but take offense when anyone disagrees with them. And they refuse to acknowledge the insights of individuals on the other side of an issue.

Let's be honest. Changing our minds is seldom, if ever, enjoyable. We can't help being a little embarrassed, even if the change occurs privately rather than publicly. Although we gain more than we lose when we exchange a weak idea for a strong one, we may feel the loss more acutely. That is understandable because we bond with opinions in much the same way that, as children, we bonded with our favorite blanket and stuffed animal. Familiar opinions provide a sense of security.

Nevertheless, changing our minds in response to evidence does not signal a lack of conviction. On the contrary, it signals courage and integrity. The key to developing this habit is to remember that *many of the ideas in our minds aren't even our own.*

All day long we receive ideas from the people around us, as well as from TV, radio, newspapers, magazines, and books. Unless we are very vigilant—and most of us aren't—false notions can take up residence in our minds. After they have been there for a while, we may be deceived into thinking they resulted from careful thinking on our part.

But what about opinions you are certain are your own? Should you be willing to change those too? Absolutely. The reason is simple: *Your opinions and convictions do not own you; you own them.* Any time you find an opinion to be lacking in quality, you have a right to discard it. If you think carefully and well, of course, many of your opinions will pass the most rigorous examination. When that happens, you can congratulate yourself. But you should be prepared to change your mind whenever new evidence is discovered.

Let's see how this process of changing one's mind works in an actual situation. For many years Jennifer considered astrology a good guide to everyday living. Her reasons were that numerous newspapers, magazines, and television treated it seriously and that many well-known, educated people used it as a guide to their decision making. But then she was involved in a discussion with someone she respected. That person asserted that astrology is not only unscientific but also illogical. Jennifer left that discussion wondering whether her view of astrology was reasonable.

Seeking more evidence, Jennifer visited the library and found a number of books and articles, some supporting astrology and others rejecting it. She also checked the Internet, and interviewed a professor of psychology and a professor of comparative religion. Finally, she consulted the Yellow Pages and called a local astrologer.

Exercise 8

On a separate sheet of paper, state your present opinion on each of the following issues and your reason(s) for that opinion. Next, consider alternative views—perhaps by going to the library, conducting interviews, or researching on the Internet—and keep a record of your sources. Then decide how reasonable your view is. If it is not as reasonable as it could be, revise it.

1. Should athletes be required to meet the same entrance standards as other students?
2. Should the federal government pass laws to prohibit pornography on the Internet?
3. Should schools or companies have policies limiting use of the Internet to school or work related activities?

After evaluating her reading and discussion, Jennifer changed her initial view. Her revised view and her supporting reasons are as follows:

Many well known, educated people believe in astrology. Even so, I think it's an ineffective guide to everyday living. One reason is that astrology is based on superstitions of a primitive time. For example, because the planet Mars appears red, it has been associated with blood and aggression. Another reason is that astrology continues to say that planets influence us at the moment of birth even though science has shown beyond question that the moment of conception is a more important time. A third reason is that astrologers offer no answer to this question: If the planets Uranus, Neptune, and Pluto were discovered after 1780, weren't all horoscopes before that time necessarily wrong?

By having the courage to change her mind when the evidence called for it, Jennifer was able to adopt a more realistic view of astrology.

A comprehensive thinking strategy

This section consolidates the principles and approaches explained in the chapter into a single thinking strategy. The strategy consists of four steps: (1) Identify facts and opinion(s), (2) Check the facts and test the opinion(s), (3) Evaluate the evidence, and (4) Make your judgment.

This strategy will work best if you create and maintain a journal of your thoughts. This will enable you to see what you are thinking. It will also expand your thinking—the act of putting ideas to paper (or computer) tends to produce more and often better ideas. Your journal may be a computer document or an actual notebook. If you choose a notebook, use the left pages for recording observations and the right pages for reflections on those observations. Be sure to leave extra space for reflections so that you can expand them.

Step 1: Identify facts and opinions

For each sentence in the paragraph or essay in question, ask these questions: *Is what is said here generally understood to be factual? Is it common knowledge or at least easily verifiable?* If the answer to both questions is "no," consider the sentence an opinion.

Step 2: Check the facts and test the opinion(s)

Investigate, as necessary, to determine whether what the person presents as facts are, indeed, facts. Be sure that he or she has not omitted any relevant facts. Then test the opinion(s) using one or more of the approaches discussed earlier in the chapter. They are:

Consider everyday experience
Consider the opinion's likely consequences
Consider the implications
Think of exceptions
Think of counterexamples
Reverse the opinion
Look for relevant research

Step 3: Evaluate the evidence

Careful, responsible authors do not merely state their opinions—they also offer evidence in support of their opinions. If the author has offered evidence, evaluate its quality and sufficiency.

Step 4: Make your judgment

Review your findings in Steps 2 and 3 and decide whether you should agree or disagree with the viewpoint in question. Caution: Be sure to make this decision on the basis of your analysis and not on your feelings or preferences. If your decision is to disagree, state the view that you believe is more consistent with the facts. (Remember that the best view may be one that combines insights from both sides of the issue.)

▶ Exercise 9

In recent years health experts have become concerned about the increasing numbers of Americans who are significantly overweight or obese. By publicizing their concerns, the experts sparked a national debate about find the cause(s) of this phenomenon. The following essay blames the fast-food industry. Read it carefully, and then apply the four-step comprehensive thinking strategy, using a separate sheet of paper.

Shame on Fast-Food Merchants

By Elena Rodriguez

Obesity is no joke. It has been linked to heart conditions, high blood pressure, sleep apnea, diabetes, and respiratory problems. And one in five Americans qualifies as obese—that is, 30 percent heavier than the normal weight for one's height. The increase in obesity among children over the last decade or so is especially alarming.

Who is to blame for this increase? To some extent, the people themselves for eating fattening foods and not getting enough exercise. In the case of children, parents share some responsibility for allowing kids to snack continuously. But a good share of the blame must go to the fast-food industry, particularly to restaurants such as McDonald's, Burger King, and Wendy's.

The fast-food industry rejects that argument, and that comes as no surprise. If the courts were to uphold it, the dollar settlements would be huge (no pun intended). Their position would be believable if they just sat between the golden arches or whatever and waited for people to walk in and place an order. But they don't do that. They ADVERTISE. Translation: they use all kinds of slogans and gimmicks to entice people in, especially young people.

Think of all the scenes of good times and friendship you have seen in fast-food ads, with trim, athletic people chattering happily or singing jingles and dancing. (Not a bulging size 3X in sight!) Think, too, of the mouth-watering pictures of burgers and fish fillets, steam rising, ketchup oozing, and the accompanying invitation to "supersize" your order. (Never a reference to mega-milligrams of salt, mounds of sugar, or artery-clogging fat!)

When you've got all those images firmly in mind, you'll realize why the fast-food industry bears the main responsibility for the current obesity problem—because their ads deceive the public.

Exercise 10

Not everyone accepts the view that the fast-food industry is to blame for the rise in obesity. For example, the following essay disputes that charge. Read the essay carefully and then apply the four-step comprehensive thinking strategy, using a separate sheet of paper. (Note: If you strongly agreed with the first essay, you will probably be tempted to reject this essay automatically. Resist that temptation and give it a fair hearing. If the author presents good reasons for changing your mind, dare to do so.)

McD's Fault? Give Me a Break

By Shandon Jackson

Time was when people were held accountable for their behavior. Now no one is. Rude, obnoxious people blame their parents for their offenses. Semi-literate ignoramuses blame their teachers. Incompetent workers blame their employers. People who destroy their lungs by smoking blame cigarette manufacturers. Given this "blame someone else" mentality, it was predictable that sooner or later overweight people would blame fast-food vendors.

The lawsuits that have been filed against fast-food restaurants are pure frivolity, totally without merit. Anyone with a smidgeon of common sense knows that fast-food is fattening and lacking in nutritional value. Restaurants shouldn't have to post signs announcing the fact, any more than stove manufacturers should have to warn buyers that hot surfaces burn.

Do fast-food advertisements make our mouths water? Of course. Ads for diamonds and Porsche convertibles tempt us, too, but so what? Sales pitches are *meant* to sell us things we may not need or may not be good for us, and they do so by exaggerating.

The Romans invented a wonderful rule to cover such cases. It's called *caveat emptor,* "let the buyer beware." That's a polite way of saying, "If someone snookered you, take a good look in the mirror, say 'shame on you' to the person who looks back, and then get on with your life." That's still good advice.

If we don't put a stop to frivolous lawsuits, before long short people will be suing their parents for depriving them of "tall genes," chocoholics will be suing Hershey for causing their skin to break out, couch potatoes will be suing sofa manufacturers for enlarging their butts, and defeated politicians will be suing the voters for frustrating their ambitions. Enough is enough.

☑ quiz

Write your answers to these quiz questions on a separate sheet of paper.

1. This book focuses on evaluating ideas and also includes some approaches for producing them. True or false?

2. Define the term *intelligence*.

3. Why is critical thinking an important skill to develop?

4. Explain the error in this statement: "I create my own truth. What I believe to be true is true for me."

5. State the principle of contradiction. Then explain how this principle aids us in critical thinking.

6. Respond to this statement: "I have a right to my opinion, so you have no business challenging it."

7. Is it useful to argue about matters of taste? Explain.

8. Changing one's mind signals a lack of conviction. True or false? Explain your answer.

9. A reason is the basis for thinking or doing something and is commonly signaled by the word "because." True or false?

10. State and briefly explain the four steps of the comprehensive thinking strategy presented in this chapter.

Answers to this quiz may be found at http://studentsuccess.college.hmco. com/students

CHAPTER **2**

Persuasive Communication

IN THIS CHAPTER:

What is persuasion? — *Persuasion is the art of getting people to give a fair hearing to ideas that differ from their own.*

How is persuasion achieved? — *Persuasion is achieved by discussing issues honestly and fairly. This section shows how.*

Strategy for persuasive writing — *This five-step strategy will help you write more persuasively.*

Overcoming errors in grammar — *Learn to recognize and avoid these common grammatical errors.*

Overcoming errors in usage — *Learn to recognize and avoid these common errors in usage.*

Strategy for persuasive speaking — *This five-step strategy will help you speak more persuasively.*

Strategy for group discussion — *This strategy will help you contribute more effectively to group discussion.*

I n Chapter One you learned to become a better thinker. Now learn how to express your thoughts more confidently and effectively. The two activities—producing insights and communicating them to others—are essential to academic, business, and personal success. There are four broad kinds of communication: description, narration (telling a story), exposition (reporting facts), and persuasion. This chapter will focus on persuasion.

What is persuasion?

Many people define persuasion as convincing others. Let's examine that view. Have you ever had someone say, in the middle of a disagreement with you, "You're so right. I see the issue clearly now. I don't know how I could have reached such a silly conclusion. Thanks for helping me see my error." You probably haven't. People don't abandon their beliefs that easily. That's why it's a mistake to think of persuasion as convincing other people that your view is right and theirs is wrong.

Here's a more realistic definition: *Persuasion is the art of getting people to give a fair hearing to ideas that differ from their own.*

Opportunities to be persuasive arise every day in the classroom, in the workplace, in the community, and in relationships with other people.

Opportunities in the classroom

Some students consider examinations the educational equivalent of a medical checkup in which instructors examine the contents of each student's mind and make a diagnosis: "Your geography 'count' is excellent" or "You are seriously deficient in sociology."

But examinations can be considered opportunities for persuasion. From this perspective, your role is active rather than passive. You have the power to shape the conclusions your instructors reach about you. In this sense, you are the teacher and they are the learners. This is especially true of essay examinations, which require more than merely circling the right answer.

Suppose you encountered the following question on a history exam: *Identify three factors that played a role in the outbreak of the Civil War. Which, in your judgment, is the most significant?* This question would be an opportunity to persuade your instructor not only that you understand the various factors, but also that you have formed a reasonable opinion about them.

Class discussions provide additional opportunities to be persuasive. Let's say your sociology class is discussing the possible relationship between divorce and juvenile delinquency. The discussion will focus not only on what the textbook author says but also on what you and the other students *think* about what the author says. Your chance to speak represents an opportunity to persuade your classmates and instructor that your view has merit.

Opportunities in the workplace

The opportunity to be persuasive in the workplace begins when you compose your résumé and continues during the job interview. The question in every interviewer's mind is "Why should I hire this person?" Your challenge is to persuade the interviewer that you are the right person for the job.

Once you are on the job, opportunities to be persuasive can occur daily, or in some cases, hourly. At this very moment, these events are happening:

- A car salesperson is finalizing a deal with a customer.
- A stockbroker is explaining to a client why a change in investment strategy is advisable.
- A customer service representative is citing reasons why an irate customer should continue doing business with the company despite an unpleasant experience.
- A telemarketer is on the phone urging someone to switch long-distance providers.
- An inventor is trying to sell her latest invention.
- A corporate official is telling stockholders why the annual report is more encouraging than it appears.

- A junior executive is presenting her idea for a new product line to her superiors.
- A supervisor is appealing to his staff for more cooperation and teamwork in the office.
- The owner of a small business is attempting to secure a business loan.
- And thousands of people are sitting face to face with their bosses and explaining why they deserve a promotion or a pay raise.

Opportunities in the community

Opportunities to persuade others also occur in your neighborhood, town, or city in roles such as Little League coach, den mother, hospital volunteer, "Big Brother" or "Big Sister," or member of a service organization or church council. In any of these roles you are bound to encounter disagreement. Even issues of seemingly slight significance can stir passions and generate spirited debate. Should Little Leaguers buy T-shirts with logos or complete uniforms? Would Friday evening or Saturday afternoon be the best time for the sale?

Community, in the larger sense, goes beyond neighborhood and municipality. As a citizen of a state, a nation, and the world, you probably have views on the social, economic, and political issues of the day, and every day brings opportunities to express your views to other people.

Opportunities in relationships

Relationships with family, friends, and coworkers offer numerous opportunities for persuasion. For example, a close friend may be considering dropping out of school after receiving a disappointing grade, or a business associate may be angry with you for a perceived offense. Perhaps someone in your family is in the habit of drinking and driving. A young child may be inconsiderate of his friends and playmates.

▥▶ Exercise 11

Describe three recent opportunities you have had to be persuasive. Comment on whether you were successful in getting a fair hearing for your ideas and, if so, why.

_____

_____

_____

_____

_____

How is persuasion achieved?

Persuasion tries to get people to consider a viewpoint that they have not previously considered or that they have examined and rejected. The presentation has to be forceful enough to demonstrate the viewpoint's merits, but not so forceful as to give offense. The solution to this dilemma is to be so honest and fair-minded that the audience is open to receive your message. Faking these qualities is not good enough—you must demonstrate that you possess them. Here is how to do so.

Respect your audience

People never respond favorably to those who disrespect them. One important way of showing respect is to give others the benefit of the doubt. Unless you have clear evidence to the contrary, assume that people who disagree with you are as honest and well-intentioned as you are.

Understand your audience's viewpoint(s)

It is not enough to be clear about your position on an issue. You must also understand the view(s) of the people you want to persuade. If you are trying to persuade one individual, you can simply ask. In the case of the friend who wants to quit school because she received a disappointing grade, ask: *Is the course required or elective? It this the first bad grade you've received in the course? Was it an exam grade or a project grade? Did you talk to your instructor about the possibility of re-taking the exam or re-doing the project? Have you explored other alternatives to quitting school, such as getting a tutor for the course?*

Your friend's answers would reveal not only the facts of the situation but her reasoning about them, and put you in a better position to persuade her not to act rashly.

When your audience is a group of people, as is often the case in classroom discussions, understanding their viewpoints is more challenging. You may not be able to question them directly. In such cases, identify the various views that have been publicly expressed and, equally important, *the reasons offered* in support of those views.

Begin on a point of agreement

Beginning your presentation on a point of agreement establishes an atmosphere of mutual respect and puts your audience at ease. In such an atmosphere, they will be more inclined to give your viewpoint a fair hearing. In contrast, beginning on a point of disagreement can make your audience defensive and reluctant to consider your ideas.

▶ Good Thinking!

The Story of Dale Carnegie

Dale Carnegie became one of the best-selling authors of all time, but he didn't start out with that goal in mind. When he graduated from college, he went to New York City in the hope of becoming an actor. To support himself, he began teaching a communications course for adults.

Carnegie quickly determined that his students' greatest needs were in "the ability to express ideas, to assume leadership, and to arouse enthusiasm among people." To help his students develop these abilities, he studied the lives of successful people, identified the principles and strategies they followed, and used their stories as teaching materials.

Over the years, Carnegie expanded and refined these teaching materials. Eventually he assembled them into a book, which he titled *How to Win Friends and Influence People*. An instant success, it has sold tens of millions of copies in thirty-eight languages.

The principles of positive relationships and successful living that Carnegie taught are surprising in their simplicity. Here is a small sampling, in his own words:

Don't criticize, condemn or complain.

Become genuinely interested in other people.

Make the other person feel important—and do it sincerely.

If you are wrong, admit it quickly and emphatically.

Try honestly to see things from the other person's point of view.

Let the other person save face.

For more information on Dale Carnegie, see Dale Carnegie, *How to Win Friends and Influence People* (New York: Pocket Books, 1990).

Acknowledge unpleasant facts and make appropriate concessions

Your first inclination may be to fill your presentation with facts that support your view and to omit facts that challenge it. Similarly, you may be inclined to portray the opposing view as totally without merit. The first inclination is intellectually dishonest; the second is foolish. Giving in to either is likely to make your presentation less effective. Whenever you try to persuade others, be sure to acknowledge *all* the facts and insights from the various viewpoints, and do so graciously and generously.

Apply the Golden Rule

This ancient rule, "Do unto others as you would have them do unto you," can be applied to persuasion in five ways: (1) If you expect your views to be given a fair hearing, give others' views a fair hearing. (2) If you expect others to provide evidence for their views, provide evidence for yours. (3) If you dislike being forced to agree, don't force others. (4) If you resent others misrepresenting your ideas, don't misrepresent theirs. (5) If you expect civility, practice civility.

Keep your expectations modest

If you expect others to change their minds immediately on reading or hearing your ideas, you are bound to be disappointed. It takes time for people to change their minds, so expect days, weeks, or even months to pass before your attempts at persuasion bear fruit. Learn to settle for

▧▶ Exercise 12

Describe a situation in which a speaker's or writer's honesty and fair-mindedness helped to persuade you or someone you know. Explain how the person demonstrated those qualities.

_____

_____

_____

_____

▧▶ Exercise 13

Describe a situation in which one or more of the qualities of persuasion mentioned above were *lacking*. Explain what happened as a result.

_____

_____

_____

_____

presenting your ideas as well as you can and hope that they will spur the other person to further reflection on the issue.

Strategy for persuasive writing

So far we have defined persuasion and identified the factors that make communication persuasive. Let's now consider a complete strategy for composing a persuasive presentation. This section will focus on persuasive *writing*. (Persuasive speaking will be covered in a subsequent section.)

The five-step strategy that follows is to be used *after* you have identified the facts and opinions, checked the facts and tested the opinions, evaluated the reasons, and taken a position on the issue. When you have finished thinking critically about the issue you will be ready for the first step in writing.

Step 1: State what you think about the issue and why you think it

What you think about the issue will be the main idea of your paper; *why* you think it will be the supporting material. Amateur writers sometimes consider it a waste of time to write these ideas out. "I know what I think and why I think it," they ask, "so why bother stating it?" The answer is that our thoughts are often less clear and precise and our reasons less substantial than we imagine them to be. Writing them down brings our thoughts into focus and gives us a chance to refine them, if necessary. It also provides a visual reminder of our purpose in writing and keeps our attention on what we are writing.

Use this format for your statement: "I think _____ because _____." The following examples illustrate this format. (The views expressed in these examples may or may not be reasonable and the reasons may or may not be valid and sufficient.)

I think *the penalties for "white collar" crime should be stiffened* because *such crime does more harm to more people than "street crime" and* because *individuals with wealth and status should be treated no differently than ordinary people.*

I think *an international effort is needed to protect the world's rainforests* because *many nations lack the power to resist logging conglomerates and* because *the depletion of the rainforests threatens to have worldwide climatic effects.*

In some cases, of course, there may be only a single reason; in others, many reasons. Be sure to express all important reasons in your statement.

Step 2: Consider how those who disagree might react to your view

Don't assume your view is so insightful that all reactions to your view will be positive. Those who disagree are sure to raise some objections. To identify your audience's objections, put yourself in their place and ask how they would react to your main idea and to each of your reasons. Write out each objection and decide whether it has merit. If it doesn't, explain why. If it does, revise your view to eliminate the objection. (If your analysis of the issue was done carefully, such revisions will usually be minor.)

In performing this step, keep in mind that if your response to a challenge is inadequate, it may prompt another objection, as the following example illustrates. Some years ago the U.S. Justice Department filed an antitrust action against Microsoft. The charge was that by bundling its Internet Explorer with Windows 98, Microsoft had gained an unfair advantage over its competitors. To prevent Microsoft from having a monopoly and to protect the public interest, the government demanded that Microsoft either remove Internet Explorer from Windows 98 or add its competitor Netscape Communications' browser.

Microsoft Chairman Bill Gates reportedly responded that the government's demand was like "requiring Coca-Cola to include three cans of Pepsi in every six-pack." That response seemed adequate. But then the government's chief antitrust agent, Joel Klein, turned the analogy back on Gates. He said that the government's demand was like asking Coca-Cola to relinquish a little space on the grocery shelves so that Pepsi, too, could be sold there.

Step 3: Arrange your ideas and write a draft of your presentation

The simplest arrangement of a persuasive presentation is as follows:
- Begin with a non-controversial statement such as an objective summary of the issue, or a brief description of a specific situation or case that illustrates the issue, or a statement of undisputed, relevant facts.
- Clearly state your main idea—your view of the issue—in a sentence or two. If you were careful and thorough in applying critical thinking to the issue, this step will not be difficult. (You may, however, want to experiment with different statements of your view to be sure you are expressing it accurately.)
- Present, in turn, each of your reasons for thinking as you do. Complete one reason before moving on to the next one, and put your best reason last because that is the place of greatest emphasis. Don't assume that others will consider your reasons *good* reasons—provide supporting evidence such as research results,

statistics, and expert testimony. Because this step is the one with the greatest potential to persuade your audience, you should give it the most attention and assign it the most space in your presentation.

• Conclude your presentation. The most obvious technique for concluding is to restate your idea. That technique is effective if your presentation is long and/or complex enough that the readers might have forgotten your main idea. In a short presentation, however, restatement may be insulting to your readers. Other, equally effective techniques of concluding include using a relevant quotation or presenting a brief anecdote. These techniques reinforce your main idea without restating it.

Follow the arrangement described above and prepare a rough draft. Do this at a single sitting without worrying about matters of style, grammar, spelling, or punctuation. Generally, your paragraphs should be a modified version of the arrangement shown here, with the introduction and the main idea statement in one paragraph and each of the reasons and the conclusion in a separate paragraph.

Step 4: Check your draft for matters of style

Read your draft critically to see where your writing style can be improved. If you read aloud rather than silently, you will be able to identify flaws you might otherwise miss.

If any of your sentences are *vague* or *confusing,* revise them to be simple and direct. If any of your sentences are too *wordy,* re-phrase them. For example, change "in the area of" to "in," "in connection with" to "about," "judging on the basis of" to "judging by," "there are many cases in which" to "often," and "made inquiry regarding" to "inquired."

If your sentences are almost equal in length, create some variety. For example, combine several short sentences into a longer one. Let's say you wrote: "I entered the discussion sure of my view. Then I listened to the other students' ideas. As a result, my view changed." You could consider this revision: "Although I entered the discussion sure of my view, when I listened to the other students' ideas, my view changed."

Another way to create variety is to change the order of phrases and clauses, being careful not to create an awkward word pattern. For example, instead of writing "I did well in the course even though I lacked the background for it," you could write, "Even though I lacked the background for the course, I did well in it."

Step 5: Check your draft for grammar, usage, punctuation, and spelling

Some computer programs check for spelling and grammar errors, but even the best ones will miss some errors, especially the use of an incorrect

▶ **Good Thinking!**

The Story of George Orwell

George Orwell was the pen name of the English author Eric Blair. Born in India, he was educated in England, then moved to Burma and worked as a police administrator. Later he fought in the Spanish Civil War.

Orwell, one of finest prose writers of the twentieth century, is best known for his novels *Animal Farm* and *Nineteen Eighty-Four*. In "Politics and the English Language," his most famous essay, he showed how bloated, lifeless expression numbs the mind and leaves us vulnerable to manipulation. He also offered these timeless rules for avoiding such language:

> *Never use a metaphor, simile, or other figure of speech which you are used to seeing in print.*
> *Never use a long word where a short word will do.*
> *If it is possible to cut a word out, always cut it out.*
> *Never use the passive where you can use the active.*
> *Never use a foreign phrase, a scientific word or a jargon word if you can think of an everyday English equivalent.*
> *Break any of these rules sooner that say anything outright barbarous.*

For more information on George Orwell, see www.k-1.com/Orwell/index.cgi/about/biography.html.

sound-alike word—for example, using *principle* in place of *principal* or *preserve* instead of *persevere*. Your best approach is to use your spell-checking program but to do your own proofreading, as well. The rest of the chapter will explain the most common errors and demonstrate how to detect and correct them.

Before we turn to that topic, however, let's address a rather obvious question: *What connection do errors in grammar, usage, punctuation, and spelling have with the subject of persuasion or the larger subject of critical thinking?* Your immediate impression may be that such errors have no connection at all; in other words, that they are merely annoyances and distractions that readers (or listeners) will overlook when they become engrossed in your ideas. That impression is mistaken.

Persuasion, as we have defined it, is the art of getting people to give a fair hearing to ideas that differ from their own. The challenge of persuading others lies in the fact that they seldom want to give such a hearing to opposing ideas. In fact, their first impulse may be to find an excuse for *dismissing* such ideas. Errors in grammar, usage, and (in the case of written communication) punctuation and spelling provide that excuse. They *invite* your audience to think, "If this person is careless about the relatively simple matter of writing and spelling correctly then his/her *ideas* are not likely to have much value." Is that assessment fair or logical? No. But it is a huge obstacle to persuasion. Overcoming that obstacle is an important step in writing and speaking persuasively.

Overcoming errors in grammar

Because of space limitations, this section and the section on errors in usage will cover only the most common errors. For further assistance in these matters, as well as punctuation and spelling, consult an English handbook. No doubt a number are available in your campus library, at a used book store, or online.

Make your subjects and predicates agree

The subject of a sentence is what you are speaking about; the verb is the main part of the "predicate"—that is, what you are saying about the subject. A singular subject requires a singular verb form; a plural subject requires a plural verb form. Here are some examples of this rule:

CORRECT: Regular *exercise maintains* muscle tone. (The subject and verb form are both singular. Don't be fooled by the "s" in *maintains*. The letter "s" forms the plural of nouns but not of verbs.)

CORRECT: Regular *exercise,* she told her students, *maintains* muscle tone. (The subject of this sentence is *exercise.* Don't be fooled by the words that separate it from the verb.)

CORRECT: All people *are* expected to attend the meeting. (*All* is plural; that is, more than one. *Are* is the plural form of the verb.)

CORRECT: Each of the people who attend *is* expected to report on his or her project. (*Each,* not *people,* is the subject and it is singular. *Is* is the appropriate singular form of the verb.)

Some plural nouns are mistakenly thought to be singular, notably *data, criteria,* and *phenomena.* (Their singular forms are, respectively, *datum, criterion,* and *phenomenon.*) Thus it would be correct to say "the criterion *is*" and "the criteria *are.*"

Other nouns, such as *audience* and *committee,* are collective. They can be considered singular (each member individually) or plural (the group as a whole). Also, some nouns have a plural form (end in "s") but are considered singular. They include *athletics, mathematics, economics, physics, measles,* and *statistics.*

Choose correct pronoun case

Pronouns are used in place of nouns. For example, instead of saying "Tom gave Mary Tom's assurance that Tom would visit Mary over the summer," you would say "Tom gave Mary *his* assurance that *he* would visit *her* over the summer." (The italicized words are pronouns.) The most common errors in pronoun case involve misusing *I* and *me, he* and *him, she* and *her, we* and *us. I, he, she,* and *we* are used as subjects of sentences or as complements after a form of the verb to be (for example, *am, is, are, was, were, will be*). *Me, him, her,* and *us* are used as direct or indirect objects, or as the objects of prepositions. Here are some examples:

ERROR: Paul suggested that *him* and *me* join the Marines. CORRECTION: Paul suggested that *he* and *I* join the Marines. (The words in question serve as the subject of the verb *join.*)

ERROR: They saved a seat for my friend and *I.* CORRECTION: They saved a seat for my friend and *me.* (The word is serving as one of the objects of the preposition *for.* Therefore the objective form *me* is required.)

Avoid sentence fragments

A sentence fragment is a group of words punctuated as if it were a sentence but incapable of standing alone as a sentence. Here are some examples of fragments, together with suggestions for correcting the mistake. The fragment in each case is italicized.

FRAGMENT: I love winter. *Although I hate driving on slippery roads.*

CORRECTION: I love winter, although I hate driving on slippery roads.

FRAGMENT: Sandy has to take her car to the garage tomorrow. *To get the front end aligned.*

CORRECTION: Sandy has to take her car to the garage tomorrow to get the front end aligned.

(Note: A fragment in response to a question is considered acceptable.)

ACCEPTABLE FRAGMENT: Will I accept her apology if she offers one? *Of course.*

Avoid mixed constructions

This error consists of starting a sentence with one construction and then shifting to another.

MIXED CONSTRUCTION: Because of his recent surgery is the reason he couldn't complete his physical education requirements.

CORRECTION: Because of his recent surgery, he couldn't complete his physical education requirements.

MIXED CONTRUCTION: By doing it this way is the fastest way to achieve our goal.

CORRECTION: Doing it this way is the fastest way to achieve our goal. OR By doing it this way, we can achieve our goal most quickly.

Make pronoun reference clear and accurate

If pronouns are not used carefully, the reader will be left wondering about the author's meaning. For example, in the sentence "When Agnes shouted at Betty, she began crying," we have no way of knowing which woman the pronoun *she* is referring to. Similarly, in the sentence, "In my college they don't allow smoking in the lobbies of classroom buildings," the pronoun *they* has no reference. (It could refer to the city fire department, the college administration, or perhaps some other group.) The problem of accuracy arises in sentences such as "Everyone on the team did their best." *Everyone* is singular and *their* plural. This error can be corrected in either of two ways: by changing *everyone* to *all team members,* or by changing *their* to *his or her.* (If the team were composed only of women, of course, you would change *their* to *her.*)

Distinguish adverbs from adjectives

The key to distinguishing between adverbs and adjectives is to understand the function of each. Adverbs modify verbs, adjectives, and other adverbs and usually answer where, when, how, or to what extent. Adverbs often (but not always) end in *–ly.* Adjectives modify nouns and pronouns—that is, they provide descriptive detail about people, places, or things.

EXAMPLES OF ADVERBS: He ate *hastily.* (*Hastily* modifies the verb *ate.*) She plays the trombone *really well.* (The adverb *well* modifies the verb play and the adverb *really* modifies *well.*) Note that it would be incorrect to say "She plays *good*" because *good* is an adjective and therefore can't modify a verb. Saying "She plays *real good*" would be the same error times two.

EXAMPLES OF ADJECTIVES: The *tall brunette* girl by the door is in my *literature* class. All the italicized words are adjectives. The first two modify the noun *girl;* the second modifies the noun *class.* Note that *literature* may also be used as a noun.

Choose proper comparatives and superlatives

Adjectives and adverbs are often used in comparisons between two people or things, or among many of them. For example, if John is six feet tall and Gerald is six feet, two inches tall we would say Gerald is *taller* than John. And if we include Francis, who is six feet, ten inches, in the comparison, we would say Francis is the *tallest* of the three. This progression—*tall, taller, tallest*—is said to be regular because the only thing that changes is the word ending. Many adjectives have this progression. For example, *dark, darker, darkest; swift, swifter, swiftest; healthy, healthier, healthiest; few, fewer, fewest.* Adjectives that change internally are said to be irregular: *many, more, most; little, less, least; bad, worse, worst.*

The progression is similar with adverbs. Regular adverbs simply add *more* or *most: sorrowfully, more sorrowfully, most sorrowfully; quickly, more quickly, most quickly; carefully, more carefully, most carefully*. Irregular adverbs change internally: *well, better, best; badly, worse, worst*. Whenever you are in doubt about the progression of an adjective or an adverb, consult a good dictionary.

Overcoming errors in usage

The following pairs of words are among the most frequently misused. As you read them, note which ones you are unfamiliar with. Re-read those several times until you are sure you understand them.

Amount, number. Use the word *amount* when referring to things not usually considered as individual units. Use the word *number* when referring to persons, places, or things usually considered as individual units. Thus, you would speak of an amount of sand, an amount of rain, but a number of people, a number of cars.

The same rule applies using the words *less* and *fewer* and the words *much* and *many*. *Less* refers to a smaller amount (less sand or rain); *fewer* refers to a smaller number (fewer people or cars). *Much* refers to a larger amount (much sand or rain); *many* refers to a larger number (many people or cars).

Between, among. Use *between* when two persons, places, or things are involved. Use *among* when more than two are involved. Thus you would say speak of an agreement *between* Bill and Mary, or one *among* Bill, Mary, and Sally.

Can, may. *Can* means able to do something, as in "He *can* run a four-minute mile." *May* means having permission, as in "*May* I leave class early today?"

Conscience, conscious. *Conscience* is a noun meaning "inner moral guide, sense of right and wrong in ethical matters." *Conscious* is an adjective meaning "mentally awake, aware."

Could have, could of. *Could have* is standard English. *Could've* is an acceptable contraction commonly used in speaking but not in writing. *Could of* is never correct. This same rule applies to *would have* and *should have*.

Each other, one another. *Each other* is used in references to two people; *one another*, in references to more than two people. Thus, it would correct to say "John and Agnes respect *each other*" and "The members of the chess club enjoyed competing with *one another*."

Lay, lie. These words are both verbs. *Lay* means "to place or put," and its progression is *lay* (present tense), *laid* (past tense), have or had *laid* (perfect tense). *Lie* means "to rest or recline," and its progression is *lie* (present tense), *lay* (past tense), have or had *lain* (perfect tense). The confusion between them is explained by the fact that the present tense of *lay* and the past tense of *lie* are identical. It is correct to say "I now *lay* [place] the book on the table," "I *laid* it there yesterday," and "I *have laid* it in the same place every day this week." It is also correct to say "I lie down now," "I lay down yesterday," "I *have lain* down for a nap every day after lunch for years." However, to say "He *laid* down for a nap" is to use the wrong verb.

Principal, principle. When used as a noun, *principal* means "the person in charge of a school." When used as an adjective, it means "main or primary," as in "The *principal* reason for attending college is the pursuit of knowledge." *Principle* is always a noun and means "rule," as in "I am learning the *principles* of economics."

Provided, providing. One meaning of *provided* is "cared for," as in "My parents provided well for our family." Another meaning is "with the provision that," as in "I'll go provided that Mary does." *Providing* means "furnishing," as in "Sam is responsible for providing refreshments." *Providing* is never an acceptable substitute for *provided*.

Reason is that, reason is because. The accepted expression is *reason is that*. The other expression is redundant because the word *reason* and the word *because* have the same meaning. Thus, you should say "*The reason* I volunteered is *that* it was my turn."

Set, sit. This pair of verbs is similar to *lay, lie* (see above). *Set* means "to place or put" and its principle parts are the same in every tense: "I set the fork down now," "I set it down yesterday," "I have set it down this way for years." Sit means "to rest or recline," and its principal parts are *sit, sat, sat*: "I *sit* in this chair," "I *sat* here yesterday," "I *have sat* here every evening since I bought the chair." To say someone "*set* down" in a chair is incorrect.

Through, threw. *Through* means "between" or "in one side and out the other." *Threw* is the past tense of the verb *throw*, as in "She *threw* the ball to her teammate."

Use, usage. *Use* may be either a verb or a noun. As a verb it rhymes with *news* and means "to employ or put into service." As a noun it rhymes with *noose* and means the "employment or application of something," such as a tool or a math formula. *Usage* is a very specialized noun and its most common use concerns language, as in "Modern English *usage* frowns on the use of slang in formal writing." The word *usage* is not an acceptable substitute for *use*—thus it is a mistake to say, "John's *usage* of his celebrity to gain favors is offensive."

Who, whom. *Who* and *whom* are pronouns referring to people. When the word will be the subject of a verb, choose *who*. Otherwise, choose *whom*. It would be correct to say, "The man *who* runs the restaurant is sitting in the next booth" because *who* is the subject of *runs* (**man** is the subject of *is sitting*). It would also be correct to say, "The man *whom* I introduced Sally to last night just came in the door" because the verbs *introduced* and *came in* already have subjects. If you were in doubt about whether to use *who* or *whom*, you could say instead, "The man that I introduced Sally to. . . ." As this example implies, the word *that* is an acceptable substitute for *whom*. However, the word *which* should never be used to apply to a person.

▨▶ Exercise 14

Following are some additional pairs/groups of words that are often confused. Look up each of pair or group in a good dictionary and, on a separate sheet of paper, explain how they differ in meaning and or/usage.

Accept/except, affect/effect, anyway/any way, awful/awfully, censor/censure/censer, flaunt/flout, healthy/healthful, imply/infer, like/as, personal/personnel, propose/purpose, real/really, regardless/irregardless, since/sense, stationary/stationery, than/then, to/too/two.

Strategy for persuasive speaking

In several ways, persuasion is more difficult in spoken than in written communication. Printed words can be studied again and again; spoken words, once uttered, are gone. Also, speaking is usually less formal and precise and therefore more easily misunderstood. Moreover, in spoken presentations the audience sees, as well as hears, the speaker and is therefore more easily distracted.

A speech has the same basic structure as a composition and, in most cases, is organized on paper before being delivered. For this reason, the first three steps in the strategy for persuasive speaking are the same as those for persuasive writing. They are: (1) State what you think about the issue and why you think it; (2) Consider how those who disagree might react to your view; and (3) Arrange your ideas and write a draft of your presentation. (See the earlier section for details.) The remaining steps for persuasive speaking are:

Step 4: Create note cards

Why speak from note cards rather than from a completely prepared speech? Because it is almost impossible for an inexperienced speaker to *read* a presentation without seeming lifeless and mechanical. If you don't have the text of the speech in front of you, you can't succumb to the temptation of reading it.

In creating your note cards, use key words rather than sentences so that you won't be tempted to read. Write large and limit the number of points per card so that you can move from point to point without lowering your head and squinting. (If you will be using visual aids, such as overhead slides or PowerPoint, be sure to add appropriate cues in your notes.)

Step 5: Rehearse using a tape or video recorder

Deliver your speech into a tape recorder—or, even better, into a video recorder—and then play it back, evaluating and taking notes. Repeat this as many times as necessary to achieve the following objectives:

Avoiding distracting verbal mannerisms. Such mannerisms include punctuating every sentence or two with meaningless expressions (e.g., uh, like, and you know) and raising or lowering your voice in the same way at the end of every sentence.

Avoiding distracting physical mannerisms. Such mannerisms include looking at the ceiling or at your notes instead of at your audience, shifting from foot to foot, or using the same gesture over and over. (To evaluate physical mannerisms, of course, you will need a videotape rather than an audiotape.)

Finishing each sentence before starting the next. It is bad enough to hear one speaker interrupt another, but it is even more frustrating to hear a speaker interrupt himself or herself. This happens much more frequently than you might imagine. Fear is a common cause; eager to finish, the speaker tries to say several things at once. The solution is to discipline yourself to give each sentence the attention it deserves.

Speaking loud enough to be heard and separating your words. The most meaningful material becomes meaningless if the speaker cannot be heard or if he or she runs words together in a way that makes people in the audience turn to one another and ask what was said.

Maintaining a moderate pace. Pace is the speed at which you speak. Most people have a tendency to speak fast when they become nervous, so you may have to speak at a pace that seems too slow in order to have it be just right. By practicing, you will be able to develop a sense of what is appropriate

Achieving vocal variety. What bores an audience most? Sameness, which suggests lifelessness. This effect occurs when the speaker's volume, pitch, pace, and inflection never change. To achieve variety, make your voice rise and fall in volume and pitch and deliver key lines a little more deliberately, lingering over the most important words. Where appropriate, pause for dramatic effect and give your audience a chance to process what you have said. These techniques are never artificial when they match the real emotion you feel for your topic.

When you make your actual presentation, stand up straight and maintain eye contact with your audience rather than fixing your gaze at the ceiling, floor, or back wall. (Yes, they can tell the difference.) Don't stare at any one person, of course; look from person to person. And above all, forget about yourself and focus on your message.

Strategy for group discussion*

Some people view discussion as competition, with one winner and many losers. As a result, they approach it combatively. They interrupt, shout, and browbeat others into submission. Others view discussion as serial monologue, with every person taking a turn at speaking but no one listening to anyone else. Neither perspective enhances discussion.

At its best, group discussion is an opportunity to share, test ideas, and generate insight. But this opportunity is possible only in a context of cooperation. In this context, participants approach discussion eager to listen as well as to speak, and they are prepared to explore all views vigorously yet fairly without anger or resentment. Persuasion becomes possible precisely because everyone is as open to being persuaded as to persuade others.

The following guidelines will help you become a valued participant in discussion:

Prepare in advance. If the discussion is scheduled in advance, spend some time planning for it. Study the lesson or meeting agenda, considering each point to be discussed. When a problem or an issue is involved, apply your thinking skills to it and be prepared to share your thoughts with others.

Anticipate disputes. When people of different backgrounds and perspectives address issues, disputes often arise. These can be beneficial to the group, as long as they are approached constructively. The key is to detach your ego from your ideas. Be energetic in presenting your views but not arrogant. Expect others to disagree with you and criticize your views. Refuse to take such criticism personally.

Leave private agendas outside. From time to time you may find yourself working in a group with someone you don't care for. You may have

---

* The section **"Strategy for Group Discussion"** is reprinted with the permission of the copyright holder, MindPower, Inc.

had trouble with the person in a past meeting or your personalities may just clash. Dislike for the person may tempt you to be disagreeable and even sarcastic. Such reactions hinder the group's efforts and make meetings unpleasant for everyone. You have an obligation to the group to give your best, so refuse to let your feelings toward anyone influence your behavior or your response to his or her ideas.

Cooperate with the leader. Keep in mind that the group leader has special obligations such as maintaining order, keeping discussion positive, and ensuring that all members are heard from and all perspectives considered. When the leader attempts to meet those obligations, be understanding and cooperative.

Listen to others. It is impossible to respond meaningfully to what others say in a discussion unless you first understand what they say, and the only way to understand is to listen attentively. To that end, whenever another group member has the floor, look at that person and be attentive, whether you agree or disagree. Don't permit yourself to be distracted by other people or your own thoughts. And avoid doing anything that causes others to be inattentive.

Understand before judging. If you are uncertain whether you understand a particular view, ask the person who expressed it. For example, say, "Ann, I'm not sure I heard you correctly. Are you saying that . . . ?" Then listen carefully to her answer. Base your evaluation on what she said rather than on careless assumptions about what she meant.

Be balanced. Many of the views expressed in discussion are of mixed quality. That is, they are partly valid and partly invalid, somewhat wise and somewhat foolish. Thus, the most reasonable response will often be to agree in part rather than to agree completely or disagree completely. To be sure your evaluation is fair, take special care to find the flaws in views you agree with and the merits of views you disagree with.

Be courteous. When views clash and discussions grow heated, it's easy to forget the rules of civility. Whenever that happens, bad feelings usually follow and group accomplishments are threatened. To avoid such outcomes, make it your habit to give no offense to others and to be slow to take offense yourself.

Monitor your contributions. Be aware of how often you contribute to the discussion. If you tend to speak a lot, make an effort to limit your contributions to matters you regard as important. On the other hand, if you seldom say anything, start contributing more often. (If others express your ideas before you get a chance to, you can always express agreement and explain your reasons.) Also monitor the *kinds* of contributions that you make to discussions. Ideally, you will propose ideas of your own *and* offer constructive criticism of other people's ideas. If all your contributions are criticisms you will be a hindrance rather than a help to the group.

Be alert for insights. When knowledgeable people exchange ideas, they often stimulate one another's thinking and produce new insights. Unfortunately, insights are often so mixed in with ordinary ideas that they go unnoticed. You will be better able to find them if you actively look for them in all contributions, other people's as well as your own.

Exercise 15

The fact that many elementary and secondary school students have learning deficiencies has prompted a search for remedies. Some people believe the problem lies with poor teaching and propose that elementary and secondary schoolteachers' salaries be based on their students' performance on standardized tests. Other people strongly object to this proposal and reject the idea it is based on. The following essays take opposing views on the issue. Read each essay carefully. Then apply to each the four-step comprehensive thinking strategy you learned in Chapter One. Use a separate sheet of paper for this exercise.

If the Student Hasn't Learned, the Teacher Hasn't Taught
By Greta Von Hoffman

Compared to their counterparts in other countries, U.S. students are mediocre academically. That's not pleasant to acknowledge, but it's been documented in international competitions for years.

To cite but one example, thirty-four nations participated in the 1999 Trends in International Math and Science Study (TIMSS) competition. U.S. students scored nineteenth in math, behind Singapore, Korea, Japan, Canada, and even behind Slovenia, Bulgaria, and Latvia. And they did only slightly better in science, scoring eighteenth.

The problem is not confined to math and science. The deficiencies of U.S. students in geography and English—their native language!—are legendary.

What could cause such embarrassing deficiencies? Not a lack of funding—the U.S. invests more money per pupil than almost any other nation. Not a lack of technology—there are more computers in U.S. schools than in any other schools in the world, with the possible exception of Japan. Surely not a national genetic deficiency.

What, then? To say it bluntly, half-hearted or downright incompetent teaching. The old saying, "If the student hasn't learned, the teacher hasn't taught," isn't just a clever slogan—it's a profound truth.

Many teachers are more concerned with collecting a paycheck than in expanding students' knowledge. Others are "hanging in" until they are eligible

➡️ ## Exercise 15 (cont.)

for retirement. Unfortunately for their students, their retirement is still ten or more years away. A considerable number of teachers have had more education courses than content courses. What good is it to know how to teach math or history or biology if you have only a nodding acquaintance with the subject of math or history or biology? It's like having a non-athlete coach a sport or someone who can't drive a car teach driver education. Watch out world.

To reform a system with such fundamental problems will not be easy. No single solution can possibly do it. That said, one small but important step would be to base teacher's pay on their performance. Teachers whose students perform exceptionally well should receive a generous pay increase. Those whose students perform poorly should receive nothing except a warning—"Produce better results or look for another job." And then—this is most important—the schools should make good on the warning.

Such a regime will encourage the good teachers, weed out the poor ones, send a message to colleges of education to prepare their students better, and invite talented people to enter the field. As I said, this isn't the entire solution, but it would be a wonderful first step.

Let's Not Scapegoat Teachers
By Pyadhammo Bikkhu

Given this country's resources, our education system should be the finest in the world. And our students' performance should be unquestionably superior to other industrialized nations. The fact that the system is badly flawed and our students are, to put it mildly, less than superior is a scandal of major proportions. No reasonable person would deny this fact.

The blame for this situation is usually placed on teachers and the standard solution is to hit them in the pocketbook as a punishment. Chief among the ideas proposed is to pay teachers according to the results they achieve—that is, the grades their students receive on national or international tests of competency.

At first thought, this all sounds very reasonable. However, it is not reasonable at all but the shabbiest kind of scapegoating. Moreover, it would be counterproductive. To begin with, students' academic deficiencies are not clearly the fault of teachers. Other candidates for blame include the school administrators, media, parents, and students themselves. Let's look at each of these groups.

Administrators have more control over what is taught and the way it is taught than most people realize. They usually have a major say in curriculum development, classroom schedules, textbook selection, and grading. Teachers are often required to spend valuable time on self-esteem, values clarification, sex education, environmentalism, and other politically correct topics, and this sharply diminishes the time they have to spend on academic subjects. Also, administrators often create a lot of bureaucratic busy work that further erodes

⬛ Exercise 15 (cont.)

instructional time. And, as if that weren't enough, when teachers attempt to maintain control of their classrooms, they get little or no support from principals and superintendents.

The media deserve a large share of the blame for student deficiencies because they have created a mass culture in which feeling good ranks above obtaining knowledge and learning self-discipline. The media also ridicule virtually every value conscientious teachers and parents try to instill in students. Not every parent is conscientious, of course, and those that aren't tend to approve and even model the harmful attitudes that block students from learning.

Finally, and every bit as important, there are the students themselves. The most admirable parents, enlightened school administrators, and dedicated teachers cannot make students learn if the students choose not to do so. And many students make that choice.

In light of these considerations, the idea of punishing teachers by taking away their salary raises is grossly unfair. Teachers' pay is already the lowest among the professions, as little as $29,000 to start in some states. That's after four years of hard work and $75,000 or so of education loans to be repaid. To expect teachers to work for such wages and have their salary advancement tied to factors over which they have no control is absurd.

For all these reasons, the idea of paying teachers according to students' performance should be tossed in the wastebasket where it belongs.

⬛ Exercise 16

In the previous exercise you analyzed two essays that addressed the question of whether elementary and secondary schoolteachers' salaries should be based on students' academic performance. Now select the essay you decided was most reasonable and evaluate it for persuasiveness, using as your guideline the strategy for persuasive writing presented in this chapter. If you see any room for improvement in persuasiveness, explain below what changes you would make.

_____

_____

_____

_____

_____

_____

▶ Exercise 17

Describe a situation in which you attempted to be persuasive, for example, a situation at work or in college. Revisit that situation, apply the guidelines for persuasion, and explain how you would approach the situation if it were occurring now. (Feel free to substitute a present situation for a past one if you wish.)

_____

_____

_____

_____

_____

_____

▶ Exercise 18

Contemporary feminism is divided into two main camps—"gender" feminism and "equity" feminism. Gender feminists include Gloria Steinem and Patricia Ireland. Equity feminists include Christina Hoff Sommers and Camille Paglia. The two camps take rather different views of the many issues of special interest to women, including the question of what the women's movement's main agenda should be. Investigate the differences between the two camps. Then decide which side you are more inclined to agree with and, on a separate sheet of paper, write a persuasive composition presenting your view. Be sure to list the sources you consulted. (Note: If you are unsure how to proceed in your investigation, see Chapter Three for help.)

☑ quiz

Write your answers on a separate sheet of paper.

1. Define persuasion as the chapter defines it.

2. Name four places where you can find opportunities to be persuasive.

3. The strategies of persuasion guarantee that you will be successful. True or false? Explain.

4. If persuasion occurs at all, it occurs immediately after you present your ideas. True or false? Explain.

5. Why is it important to eliminate errors in grammar and usage from your persuasive writing and speaking?

6. The challenge of persuading others is greater in spoken communication than in written communication. True or false? Explain.

7. People who are quiet by nature should be content to let others talk during group discussions. True or false?

8. In grammar the term *mixed construction* means mixing foreign phrases with English. True or false?

9. In what ways is persuasive speaking more difficult than persuasive writing?

10. List the five steps for persuasive writing.

Answers to this quiz may be found at http://studentsuccess.college.hmco. com/students.

CHAPTER 3

Becoming an Individual

IN THIS CHAPTER:

What is individuality? — *Individuality is the quality or qualities that set one person apart from others.*

Acknowledging influences — *The first step in becoming an individual is to admit that other people have shaped you.*

Understanding attitudes — *Attitudes are beliefs that are expressed indirectly, for example through tone of voice, mannerisms, or actions.*

Four empowering attitudes — *These attitudes will help you become a critical thinker and make you more successful in all your endeavors.*

Recognizing manipulation — *Common devices of manipulation include biased reporting, dishonest appeals to emotion, stacking the deck, suppressing dissent, and repetition.*

Resisting manipulation — *This four-step approach will help you resist being manipulated by others.*

Habits for individuality — *These habits provide you with an additional way to become more of an individual.*

What is individuality?

The term *individuality* is easily defined: it is the quality or qualities that set one person apart from others. However, the question of when and how a person becomes an individual is a little harder to answer. The popular notion is that we are all individuals from conception and anything we think, say, or do expresses our individuality. Let's examine this idea to see if it makes sense.

If everyone were unique, imitation would be rare. Indeed, it might not exist at all. We'd find little similarity in dress, speech patterns, and mannerisms, let alone viewpoints. Yet even a casual glance at people reveals a different picture.

Count the number of young men's feet in unlaced high top sneakers. Tally the number of designer labels on male or female jeans. Notice how many businessmen wear suits, shirts, and ties in the current style. See how many businesswomen have hemlines precisely where this year's fashion experts declared they should be.

Note speech patterns, observe mannerisms, and listen to opinions on issues from abortion and capital punishment to taxation and welfare reform. You're likely to see much more sameness than difference.

Such observations suggest that the popular notion of individuality is shallow. People are not born with individuality but with the potential to develop it. Likewise, people's actions and words may not express individuality at all but mindless conformity. In short, individuality takes effort.

▶ **Good Thinking!**

The Story of Viktor Frankl

Viktor Frankl (1905–1997), a renowned Viennese psychiatrist, was influenced by two older Viennese psychiatrists, Sigmund Freud and Alfred Adler. Freud believed the sex drive is the strongest psychological drive in human beings; Adler believed it is the drive for power.

But Frankl eventually formed a different view—that the strongest drive in human beings is the drive to find meaning in life. His evidence came not only from the psychiatrist's couch but also from his experiences as an inmate in Nazi concentration camps where his wife, father, mother, and brother perished.

The experience of camp life included near-starvation, lack of warm clothing, disease, hard labor, and unspeakable brutality. In such conditions, Frankl found, the sex drive and the drive for power were quickly suppressed. But the drive to find *meaning* in the suffering, a reason for living, remained strong.

Amid the horrors of the camps, many inmates put aside selfishness and displayed compassion and kindness toward their fellow inmates. Some even forgave their captors.

Frankl survived the camps, largely because of his determination to tell the stories of decency and nobility he witnessed and to teach others the lessons he learned about finding meaning in one's life, regardless of one's circumstances.

The best known of Viktor Frankl's books, *Man's Search for Meaning,* presents these stories and lessons. To date more than nine million copies are in print in numerous languages.

For more information on Viktor Frankl, see Viktor Frankl, *Man's Search for Meaning*, 3d ed. (New York: Simon & Schuster, 1984), or www.empirezine.com/spotlight/frankl/frankl1.htm.

Acknowledging influences

The first step in becoming an individual is to admit that other people have shaped you. There's no shame in this—it is an unavoidable consequence of living in society. When we were children, we learned by imitating other people. This happened first with our parents and relatives and later with our teachers and peers. The way we think and speak and act, even today, naturally reflects those childhood lessons. And though our imitation is less conscious and obvious in adulthood, it is no less real.

Another powerful influence is the popular culture disseminated by the communications and entertainment media, notably television. During our formative years, most of us saw thousands of hours of television. Small children have difficulty distinguishing between commercials and program content, so we no doubt gave the claims of used car salespeople the same trust we gave the weather reports. In time we learned that not all the people who appear on the screen are equally believable. Yet by then most of us had become accustomed to relaxing our minds while watching TV, so we remained—and remain—vulnerable to the influences of other people.

Over the years those influential people have numbered in the thousands. They include the screenwriters who created TV dramas and comedies, the actors who brought the scripts to life, the newscasters who reported the news, and the pundits and commentators who told us what it meant. Those people may have intended to do nothing more than entertain or inform us. But, whatever their intentions, they were also planting ideas and shaping our thinking and behavior in subtle but significant ways.

Suppose that you open today's newspaper and the headlines say that a well-known person led a protest march, a politician resigned in disgrace, and a snowstorm blanketed the Midwest.

You may take it for granted that those stories represent the most important events that occurred in the past twenty-four hours. But stop and think about that. The editors who selected those stories have their own ideas of what is newsworthy, and their ideas may be debatable.

For example, many editors follow the principle, "If it bleeds, it leads," which may not be the most responsible principle to follow. Consider, as well, that in choosing their stories, editors also chose to ignore many other stories. Did you read about the historic conference in Washington, D.C., featuring a Catholic priest, a Protestant minister, a Black Muslim, a Hindu, a Rabbi, and a Buddhist talking about their common spiritual and social values? (This event took place in November 2000.) Chances are you didn't hear about it because most editors around the country decided it wasn't newsworthy.

The same pattern exists in book and magazine publishing. Authors are free to take any view they want about any subject. But what editors select for publication is what they think the public should know or what will sell.

Given all these influences, it is almost certain that many of the ideas, attitudes, and values you consider your own actually came from other people. "Wait a minute," you may be saying. "How could I ever mistake other people's ideas for my own?" The following sequence of events illustrates how this happens.

You're watching your favorite TV series and one of the characters expresses an offhand opinion about a controversial issue, but you don't pay much attention because you have little interest in the issue and you are busy concentrating on the story line. A few days later, you are listening to a radio talk show while doing some chores and you hear someone express the same opinion. It sounds familiar to you, but you are too involved in what you are doing to think further about it.

The following week you're sitting with a couple of friends and the discussion turns to the very same issue. Your friends disagree about it and then ask you where you stand. Not wanting to admit that you haven't really thought much about it, you say the first thing that comes to mind—the opinion you heard others express.

Once you express the opinion, of course, you stop thinking of it as *an* opinion—it becomes *your* opinion, the *right* opinion. And the more often you express it, the more convinced you will be of its soundness, and the more passionate you will be in defending it. *All this for an idea you never examined critically but merely heard others say!*

Acknowledging that you have been—and continue to be—influenced by other people will motivate you to be more critical of your own ideas and more willing to reject them when they prove unworthy. It will also help you to appreciate the wisdom in C. M. Ward's observation: "There are times when the greatest change needed is a change of my viewpoint."

⏩ Exercise 19

On a separate sheet of paper make a list of the people who have most influenced you and the specific effects their influence has had (example: "my mother's warnings made me suspicious of strangers"). Aim to identify some less obvious influences, including some that you have never recognized before (example: your imitation of the dress and manner of a celebrity).

Understanding attitudes

Attitudes are beliefs that are expressed indirectly, for example through tone of voice, mannerisms, or actions. We are seldom as aware of our attitudes as we are of our other beliefs. Some people have the attitude that they are more important than other people. They may never say to anyone, "I am more important than you," and perhaps they don't even think those words to themselves, but the attitude is expressed in the way they treat other people. For example, they may demand kindness, sensitivity, and loyalty from others but never reciprocate; they may break dates or change plans whenever they wish but resent their friends doing so; or they may expect apologies but never offer them.

Our attitudes are strongly influenced by our culture—that is, by the moral code, religious beliefs, political perspective, and social customs we were introduced to at home and in our community. There is nothing mystical about this influence. It can be explained by the fact that cultures differ in the behaviors they approve and disapprove and in the strength of their convictions about those behaviors.

It is well known that students in many Asian countries have a more respectful attitude toward parents and teachers than American students typically have. Some observers believe this attitude is responsible for the unusually high level of academic achievement among Asian students. Similarly, the Old Order Amish have a stricter moral and social code than most other Americans and, perhaps not coincidentally, a much lower incidence of crime.

Over the last half-century, a new kind of culture—*popular* culture—has emerged in a number of western countries, particularly in the United States. The entertainment and communications media disseminate this popular culture, and its values are very different from those of traditional culture. The result has been a "culture war" that popular culture seems to be winning.

Consider, for example, the changes in the public's attitude toward sex and violence in media. Traditionally, most people strongly opposed the use of vulgar language and graphic depictions of sex and violence. Audiences were offended when "damn" was used in *Gone with the Wind*. Navels had to be covered in shows such as *I Dream of Jeannie*. Depictions of two people in bed, even a married couple, were outlawed for decades.

Then filmmakers and television writers began to push limits by breaking one taboo after another. As such material became more common and familiar, the public's attitude changed. Today many people not only tolerate but expect—in some cases *crave*—a steady diet of the scandalous and the sensational. And not just from dramatic shows but also from the news! This change is but one indication of popular culture's powerful influence on our attitudes.

Evaluating your attitudes is an important step in becoming a critical thinker. Before you can decide whether your attitudes are responsible and beneficial you must identify them. And doing so can be difficult if you are not aware that you have them. The following exercises are designed to help you identify your attitudes about some matters important in college, at work, and in personal relationships.

▶ Exercise 20

PART I

Record your first thought about each of the following subjects in the space provided. Respond directly and honestly. *Don't screen out any ideas or change them to fit what you think others might want you to say.* If you turn in these exercises, be sure to save them when your instructor returns them to you.

Keeping promises

I try my best to keep promises
positive

Being on time

I do not like to be the first eager one there so I am always a few mins. late

Manners

I believe in good manners + apologize reuse myself often.   beneficial

Personal appearance

At work - look as corp. chic as possible
At home - relax + let your hair down even when you have guest.

Success in life

I am successful if my kids become successful. Family comes first + work is a way to provide for family comforts.   positive

Parents, teachers, employers

I respect all parents + teachers. Employers are to be treated w/ dignity.   beneficial

Exercise 20 (cont.)

Free speech

Love it   *positive*

Discipline

I do believe in disciplining my children. I am not as disciplined w/ myself as I want to be.   *beneficial*

Apologizing

So often its meaningless.

Excellence

I expect myself to try hard + do my best.   *positive*

PART II

Now evaluate what you recorded in Part I. In each case decide whether your reaction is positive, constructive, and beneficial. If it is not, explain what reaction would be better. Write your evaluation next to each entry.

 Exercise 21

Have you ever made, or heard others make, any of the following statements? If so, describe the occasion. Then identify the attitude each statement suggests.

"This course doesn't matter because it's not required for my major."

▶ Exercise 21 (cont.)

"This instructor is assigning too much work."

Yes

"It's only fair for the instructor to put something on the test if she said we were responsible for knowing it."

"If the class gets too tough, I'll drop it."

No

"The reason I'm doing poorly is that the teacher doesn't like me."

Yes

"Students who take part in class discussions are just trying to impress the teacher."

No

▶ Exercise 22

Describe your reactions to the following situations—that is, what you would typically think, say, and do. Then identify the attitude that prompts that response.

You express a point of view in a conversation and a friend disagrees with you.

Frustrated. Have to work harder to make a point.

You're in a large class and the teacher calls on you.

No fear. Try to answer question

▶ Exercise 22 (cont.)

You're doing a homework assignment and are unsure how to proceed.

You're listening to someone you don't like. He's talking to a group of your friends, and they seem interested in what he's saying.

Listen as well. I want to find out where his mind is at.

You begin reading a book or an article on a subject you feel strongly about. Then you realize the author's view strongly opposes yours.

Keep reading!

Four empowering attitudes

We have discussed what attitudes are and how they are acquired, as well as how you can identify and evaluate your own attitudes. Now let's consider some specific attitudes that can help you become a critical thinker and make you more successful in your studies, your career, and your personal life.

Attitude 1: There's always room for improvement

For centuries most people believed that human beings are imperfect creatures and no matter how far they advance toward perfection, there will always be room for improvement. This belief was the foundation of the concept of self-improvement. But, over the last few decades, something strange happened. Self-improvement books and tapes began to focus less on *improving* and more on *approving*. Self-acceptance became the dominant theme. Some authors even advised us to chant "I'm wonderful just as I am," "I'm perfect," even "I'm divine." They told us if we acknowledged our imperfections or faults, we'd suffer a fatal loss of self-esteem.

These authors overlooked a crucial fact of life—*people never strive to obtain what they believe they already have.* Only a foolish person would waste time fixing what isn't broken.

If you believe you are already filled with knowledge, understanding, and wisdom, you probably aren't enthusiastic about your studies. Similarly, if you believe you have no personal faults—rudeness, selfishness, or meanness, for example—you probably spend little time wondering whether you have acted inappropriately. Instead, you assume that if other people take offense at something you say or do in school, at work, or in your personal life, there must be something wrong with *them*.

The moment you admit to yourself that you haven't accomplished all you have the potential to accomplish, and that you aren't all you could be as a person, you'll become more open to improvement.

Attitude 2: Criticism, including self-criticism, has value

The same influential people who claim that we are already wonderful also advise us to reject criticism from other people and even from ourselves. Many of us follow this advice and assume that anyone who criticizes us is disrespecting (in popular parlance, "dissing") us. We expect total acceptance from other people; that is, unqualified agreement with what we say, and praise for what we do. And if we don't get it, we are offended.

Such an attitude is unrealistic. Think of any learning situation you have been in; for example, learning how to ride a bike, drive a car, play a team sport, write an essay, or perform a new procedure at work. In all of these cases, you probably had a parent, teacher, coach, or mentor saying "No, that's not the way," and offering suggestions for doing it right. (Even if you learned by yourself, you told yourself something similar.)

If you rejected the criticism, you probably had difficulty learning. In fact, you may not have learned at all. Athletic coaches describe people in the latter category as "uncoachable" and often drop them from the team, even if they have significant athletic potential. On the other hand, if you put aside ego, accepted the criticism, and followed the advice, you probably learned faster and better.

Do some people criticize too much or do so in an inappropriate way? Yes they do, and the best way to deal with this is to accept only the valid part of the criticism and ignore the rest. Can *self*-criticism be carried too far, to the point that paralyzes effort? Yes again, but this consequence can be easily avoided. Just keep your self-criticism focused on the positive goal of doing better next time.

Attitude 3: Effort is the key to success

Many people have the attitude that success is solely dependent on talent. For example, when others get better grades in college, they think, "I wish I were that smart." When they see accomplished athletes perform, they say, "It must be nice to have such natural ability." When they read of people who have been successful in business, the professions, or the arts, they say, "I wish I had their gifts."

That attitude is mistaken. Talent is a factor in performance but it is not the only factor. Two others are desire and effort. Moreover, these two are more important because *you can control them*. People with only modest talent who really want to learn something and are willing to work hard often surpass more talented people who lack their desire and initiative. And with achieving a hard-earned goal comes the exciting realization that their talent was greater than they imagined.

According to Thomas Edison, one of the greatest inventors of all time, "Genius is 1 percent inspiration and 99 percent perspiration." Making this your attitude will bring out the best that is in you and, in the process, produce the healthiest kind of self-esteem—*earned* self-esteem.

Attitude 4: Other people are as important as I am

Modern culture has conditioned us to be more concerned with rights than with responsibilities. Given this emphasis, it is understandable that many people who believe they should be treated well feel no obligation to treat others similarly.

In sharp contrast to this self-serving attitude is the attitude embodied in the traditional view of the "gentleman," as expressed in the following quotations from *A Gentleman's Code According to Confucius, Mencius, and Others.*

> A gentleman daily examines his personal conduct on three points: In carrying out the duties entrusted to him by others, has he failed in conscientiousness? In dealing with his friends, has he failed in sincerity and faithfulness? In all his dealings, has he failed to pass on whatever he has learned which may assist others?—*Confucius*

> A true gentleman helps others to realize what is good in them; he does not help others to discover their weaknesses and failings. —*Confucius*

> A gentleman sets strict standards for himself, but makes allowances for others.—*Confucius*

> A gentleman tries to banish from his bearing all traces of violence and arrogance, to remove from his actions all insincerity, to purge from his speech all vulgarity and impropriety.—*Confucius*

> A gentleman is one who thinks more of other people's feelings than his own rights; and more of other people's rights than his own feelings.—*Matthew Henry Buckham*

> One of the marks of a gentleman is his refusal to make an issue out of every difference of opinion.—*Arnold H. Glasgow*

> This is the final test of a gentleman; his respect for those who can be of no possible service to him.—*William Lyon Phelps*

> . . . It is almost a definition of a gentleman to say he is one who never inflicts pain.—*John Henry, Cardinal Newman*

All these quotations embody the attitude that other people are as important as we are and therefore deserving of the same level of respect we wish for ourselves. Far from being a mark of weakness, this attitude will gain you respect and admiration.

Recognizing manipulation

Manipulation is a form of influencing. What distinguishes it from other forms is that it uses *dishonest* means. Among the most common of those means are biased reporting, dishonest appeals to emotion, stacking the deck, suppressing dissent, and repetition. Let's look at each in turn.

Biased reporting

A number of books have been written on the subject of biased reporting, including *Bias* and *Arrogance* by Bernard Goldberg and William McGowan's *Coloring the News*. But the book that provides the most useful insights is Bob Kohn's *Journalistic Fraud*. Kohn focuses his analysis on a single newspaper, the *New York Times,* because it has long been regarded as the "journal of record" and because it is the single most influential news source in the western world. In this country alone, more than 650 other newspapers subscribe to the *Times's* news service, and many broadcast news organizations lean heavily on its news reports.

As Kohn notes, codes of journalistic ethics used to require that opinion be confined to the editorial page. A 1923 code stated: "News reports should be free from opinion or bias of any kind." A journalism textbook written the same year taught that "a news article should tell what happened in the simplest, briefest, most attractive and accurate manner possible; it should draw no conclusions, make no gratuitous accusations, indulge in no speculation, give no opinions." For years, the *New York Times* endorsed that standard, promising to "give the news impartially, without fear or favor, regardless of party, sect or interests involved."

According to Kohn, the *Times,* and many other news agencies, no longer follow that standard. As a result, much of today's news unfairly favors the particular news agency's or individual reporter's point of view. Such bias can take a variety of forms, notably the following:

Biased headline. Let's say the Senate votes 93 to 7 in favor of a health care bill. A fair headline would be "Senate Passes Health Care Bill." A reporter or editor who disapproved of the vote might substitute this biased headline: "Opinion Divided on Health Care Bill."

Biased "lead." The term *lead* refers to the opening sentence or sentences of a news story. A fair lead simply states who did what, as well as when and where the event occurred. An unfair lead injects opinion in an attempt to influence the reader's reaction to the news. For example, if a government commission issued a proposal and the reporter didn't like it, he or she might begin, "In a move sure to create controversy . . . ." The bias in this case is that instead of reporting, these words predict a future event which may or may not occur.

Biased reporting of polls. Fair reporting is evenhanded in presenting the results of polls. In contrast, biased news reporting is inconsistent. If the news agency agrees with the results, it puts the story on the front page. If it disagrees, it buries the story or, in extreme cases, omits it altogether. In some instances, a news organization will itself commission a poll or study and, when the results are disappointing, decline to publish it.

Biased handling of quotations. Readers have a right to expect that the quotations used in news stories will fairly depict the range of viewpoints on the subject. Unbiased reporters strive to meet that standard. However, biased reporters try to advance their own personal opinions. One way is to include numerous strong quotations on their side of the issue and only one or two, preferably weak quotations on the other side. A more blatant approach is to include *no opposing quotations* at all and thus create the impression that no responsible person would take the opposing side of the issue. The most dishonest approach is to twist a quotation so that it seems to say something very different. For example, if the quotation were "I initially had some reservations about the program, but after examining it closely I believe it is excellent," a dishonest reporter might merely say that the person expressed "some reservations" about the program.

Even journalists who sincerely desire to report objectively are sometimes tricked into using biased material. As former activist Tammy Bruce explains in her book *The New Thought Police,* reporters get much of the information they use in their news accounts from "the press releases sent to them by publicists, activists, and politicians." According to Bruce, such people don't even call the propaganda they write "press releases" any more. They call them "news releases" to make them sound like objective information.

Keep in mind that biased reporting is not limited to one political, religious, or philosophical perspective. It is no less manipulative if done by people on your side of the issue than if done by people on the other side.

Dishonest appeals to emotion

We react to language not only with our intellects but also with our emotions. Some words evoke emotion more than others. For example, we react more emotionally to "home" and "family" than to "state" or "government"; to "values" and "beliefs" more than to "concepts" or "ideas"; to "freedom" and "liberty" more than to "constitutional guarantees."

Emotional language has great value—it has the power to elevate our vision, reinforce important principles, and inspire responsible action. Virtually all of the great writers and speakers in history have used emotional language for such purposes, and we are fortunate for that. Without such language, communication would be mechanical, lifeless, dull, and ineffective.

Unfortunately, emotional language can also be used to manipulate us. Devious people would prefer to have others accept what they say uncritically and to act in conformity with their wishes. They choose language to elicit positive emotional responses to ideas and people they support and negative emotional responses to those they oppose. Such attempts at deception can be found in every area of life, but they are especially prominent in politics. Former White House advisor Dick Morris says that today's political speeches are like collections of "greatest hits"—the speakers do studies to find out what they public wants to hear and then say it.

It is not always easy to tell when an appeal to emotion is dishonest. However, you can be reasonably sure that it is dishonest when writers or speakers *routinely* use highly favorable terms to describe their side of the issue and highly unfavorable ones for the opposing side. Dishonest speakers will call people who agree with their position "moderate," "centrist," "progressive," or "pragmatic" and call people who disagree "radical," "extremist," "divisive," or "partisan." Deceptive writers will excuse serious mistakes by leaders they approve of while condemning minor mistakes in others and ascribe high intelligence and noble motives to those who agree with them, and low intelligence and devious motives to those who disagree.

Stacking the deck

The term *stacking the deck* derives from card games in which the dealer arranges the cards to cheat one or more of the players. This form of manipulation often occurs on TV talk shows about controversial issues.

A typical format features a host and two guests with different views of an issue. Fairness demands that the host remain neutral and give each guest an equal opportunity to present his or her case. Sometimes, however, the host will become a participant in the discussion, thus creating a two-against-one situation. Even more unfair is the practice of choosing guests of unequal stature and ability—in other words, inviting a well-known, highly accomplished person to represent the favored view and a relative unknown to represent the unfavored view. If, by chance, the relative unknown seems to be getting the better of the discussion, the host will give him or her less time to speak.

Suppressing dissent

For all its deviousness, stacking the deck at least acknowledges that there is an opposing view. Suppressing dissent, on the other hand, creates the impression that *there is no opposing view.* A good illustration of the effectiveness of this technique is a personal experience Tammy Bruce describes in *The New Thought Police.*

Bruce is a gay feminist who was once the President of the Los Angeles chapter of the National Organization for Women (NOW). In her ten years as an activist, she had no difficulty getting her essays published in the *Los Angeles Times.* Whatever she submitted was always accepted.

Then Bruce became disturbed at what she perceived to be the unfair treatment of Dr. Laura Schlessinger by other gay activists. She composed a short commentary expressing that view. The *Times* held it for three weeks and when she called to ask what was happening, she found an editor had decided not to publish it, essentially because it was on the "wrong" side of the issue. Next, Bruce submitted the commentary to the *New York Times* where she got an enthusiastic reception. However, they edited it in such a way that it was against Dr. Laura rather than for her. She refused to accept the changes, so the commentary was never published.

The newspapers' refusal to publish Bruce's commentary as she wrote it amounted to a suppression of dissent. As a result, readers of those newspapers were led to believe, erroneously, that no one in the gay community supported Dr. Laura.

Repetition

One of the simplest and most effective techniques of manipulation is simple repetition. The more familiar an idea is, the more people tend to believe it. Realizing this, spinmeisters and hucksters repeat their lies and distortions over and over to trick us into accepting them. Of course, honest people also repeat what they believe to be true. In either case, we have to decide whether what is repeated is true.

For example, when the Monica Lewinsky scandal occurred during the Clinton administration, the President's supporters kept repeating, "He shouldn't be impeached because his lies were only about sex." And during the election campaign of 2004, Senator John Kerry's opponents kept repeating, "It's impossible to tell where he stands because he takes *both* sides of every issue." In both cases, the people who made these statements were trying to persuade others. The public had to decide whether either, both, or neither of these statements were honest persuasion or manipulation.

Exercise 23

On a separate sheet of paper, list some examples of manipulation. Include, if you can, one example of each type discussed above. The examples may be from past or present experience.

Resisting manipulation

Given the number of individuals and groups eager to manipulate you and the many means at their disposal, it is important to have an active strategy for resisting their efforts. The following strategies are especially helpful:

Step 1: Be prepared

Manipulation does the greatest harm when you are unaware it is occurring. Therefore, the surest way to avoid its influence is to *expect to encounter it* whenever you read a book, magazine, or newspaper, whenever you see a movie or TV show, and whenever you listen to the radio, visit the Internet, or engage in a discussion. This doesn't mean you need to be suspicious of everyone, just be aware that misinformation and lies can be spread in much the same way that computer viruses are spread—by honest people who have themselves been fooled.

Being prepared means remaining alert for signs of manipulation. For example, when you read or watch the news, look for biased reporting. And when you watch a talk show (or even a drama or sitcom), look for dishonest appeals to emotion, stacking the deck, and repetition. Suppression of dissent is hardest to detect. Instead of looking for what is present, you must look for what is absent—that is, what has been purposely *omitted*. Keep in mind that there are two (or more) sides to every controversy. Whenever you are presented with only *one* side, you may reasonably conclude that the other has been suppressed.

Step 2: Ask questions

We all start out life with abundant curiosity. Because everything is new to us, we are filled with wonder and constantly asking questions, especially "What is that?" "Why is it that way?" and "What does it mean?" Unfortunately, our parents and teachers get tired of answering, so we stop asking and our curiosity eventually shrivels.

Happily, curiosity can be reactivated. Begin by forcing yourself to ask probing questions about what you see and hear. Do so with everyday matters as well as with controversial situations. In time, wondering will become a habit. Here are some sample situations and kinds of questions you might ask:

THE SITUATIONS

You are sitting with some friends in the campus cafeteria. One of your friends is expressing dissatisfaction. She says: "*I'm disappointed with the instructors at this college—they seem content to offer uninteresting courses. For example, they stand at the lectern and lecture all period without enthusiasm for their material. On the rare occasions when they open discussion to the class, they call on the same few students. The rest of us have to sit squirming, waiting for the boring ordeal to be over.*"

THE QUESTIONS

As she is speaking, ask yourself these questions: *How likely is it that your friend knows all or most of the instructors at this university? How likely is it that all or most of the instructors teach strictly by lecture and without enthusiasm? Why are the same few students always called on* (assuming this claim is accurate)? *Do these students raise their hands and show an interest in the questions? Do other students, including your friend, ever volunteer a comment or question? Are all but a few students at this*

The Situations (continued)

The Questions (continued)

college really so bored, or is your friend projecting her reaction on them? Is it possible that the students who squirm have overly negative attitudes? Is it the instructor's responsibility to make a class interesting? Do the students bear any responsibility?

While driving through a rather rundown neighborhood, you pass a house with a sign advertising psychic services. It reads: "*Madam X. Palm readings, Tarot cards, Your future foretold!*"

As you drive by, ask yourself: *What could a psychic accomplish if she used her powers to better herself? Wouldn't she be able to make a fortune at the racetrack or in the stock market or the lottery and afford to live in the most exclusive section of town? So why isn't she living in a better section of town? Could it be that she has too much integrity to use her powers for her own advantage? Might she instead be a charlatan?*

While reading the newspaper, you notice this advertisement: "*Good news! Due to the unprecedented success of our giant end-of-year furniture sale, we have extended it for ten days.*"

You pause in your reading and ask yourself: *How would the store have looked after a successful sale? Would the stock be noticeably depleted? Would the store be empty of furniture? If they did sell most of the furniture, why do they need to extend the sale? And where are they getting the furniture for the extended period? Was the sale, instead, such a flop that they were left with a store full of merchandise and they have to extend the sale to get rid of it? If so, why didn't the furniture sell? Were the prices too high? Is the quality too low? How do competitors' prices compare?*

The Situations (continued)

You are reading a magazine article about the violence that sometimes occurs at heavy metal rock concerts. The author says that it's unfair to blame the violence on the musicians or the music, and then asserts that human beings are naturally violent.

The Questions (continued)

You ask yourself: *What other kinds of musical events might be compared with heavy metal rock concerts? Square dances, polka or bluegrass festivals, Natalie Cole concerts, or operatic performances? Have I ever seen a newspaper headline such as "Riot Mars Pavarotti Performance" or "Rowdy Polka Contestants Attack Bystanders"? If violence is due to human nature, then shouldn't it be found in all societies and all groups within a society? How common are incidents of group violence in Europe, Asia, or Africa? For that matter, how common is violence among Amish groups in the United States?*

Exercise 24

On a separate sheet of paper, identify a recent situation involving something you saw, heard, or read that you might have probed more deeply. Ask appropriate questions about the situation in the manner shown above. (Note: The next exercise will build on this one.)

Step 3: Be imaginative

Two ways to be imaginative were illustrated in Step 2. One was **creating a mental picture** of how the store would look after a successful sale. The other was **producing relevant examples**—the examples of the racetrack, stock market, and lottery in one situation, and musical events, newspaper headlines, and comparisons with Europe, Asia, and the Amish in the other situation.

Another way to be imaginative is to **create realistic scenarios.** Suppose the issue in question is whether or not television has had a harmful effect on communication in families. Here are three realistic scenarios you might imagine:

1. It's dinner time and the family is gathered at the dining room table. The television set is positioned so that everyone can see. All eyes are glued to the set. The only sounds that can be heard, other than those coming from the TV, are the occasional comments: "Pass the potatoes," "Is there any more meat in the kitchen?" At one point someone says, "Guess what happened to me today?" And everyone else says in unison, "*Sshhhh.*"

2. It's dinner time and the family is gathered in the living room, each behind a TV tray. No one looks at or speaks to the others.

3. Dinner is over, the dirty plates are in the dishwasher, and each member of the family has headed to a different corner of the house and his or her own TV set.

These scenarios would suggest questions and insights about the effect of television on communication in families.

A fourth way to be imaginative is to **construct a new viewpoint.** This approach works well in situations in which you are being pressured to adopt one of two positions on an issue, neither of which is completely satisfactory. For example, let's look at the issue of whether the Ten Commandments should be displayed in public school classrooms.

The "Pro" viewpoint: The Ten Commandments SHOULD be displayed because they are honored in two of the world's great religions, Judaism and Christianity; they express the religious and moral sentiments of the vast majority of Americans; and they provide an ethical dimension that many think has been sadly lacking in recent decades.

The "Con" viewpoint: The Ten Commandments SHOULD NOT be displayed because they are not honored by people of other faiths and those of no faith; their presence in the classroom would give favored status to Judaism and Christianity, status the Constitution forbids; and the ethical dimension the Commandments provide is necessarily a form of religious doctrine.

By being imaginative, you could construct the following new view to be compared with the other views in Step 3:

The Ten Commandments SHOULD be displayed, *along with any similar codes from other religious or philosophical traditions, including agnostic or atheistic,* **because knowledge of the principles which have guided human conduct in various times and places is as valuable as knowledge of diverse cultures and customs and because the display of many codes would favor none.**

▶ Good Thinking!

The Story of Nellie Bly

Her real name was Elizabeth Cochrane and she was born in 1867 in Pennsylvania. When she was six years old her father died and her mother had to raise Elizabeth and her fourteen brothers and sisters by herself. At sixteen Elizabeth moved to Pittsburgh to find work. One day in 1885 she read a newspaper article advancing the traditional argument that "a woman's place is in the home." She wrote a response which so impressed the editor that he hired her. She then took the name Nellie Bly and began her remarkable career.

Nellie had an active, inquiring mind that served her well in her specialty, investigative reporting. She wrote articles on marriage and divorce, and helped to initiate important legal reforms. She traveled in Mexico and wrote about exposing the political corruption and widespread poverty. She had herself committed to a New York asylum for ten days so that she could expose the terrible conditions and the inhumane treatment of the inmates. Later she traveled around the world hoping to set a new speed record. (She succeeded.)

Nellie left journalism to marry an industrialist. When he died ten years later, she took over control of his company and won praise for her enlightened treatment of her employees. At a time when workers typically labored long hours in unhealthy sweatshops for low pay, she provided her workers with health care, libraries, and gymnasiums.

Eventually, Nellie returned to reporting. While she was on holiday in Europe, the First World War broke out, and she immediately volunteered to be a war correspondent for the *New York Journal*. She became the first female correspondent to cover a war from the front lines. After the war, Nellie returned home and wrote a newspaper column until her death of pneumonia in 1922.

For more information on Nellie Bly, see http://az.essortment.com/ nellyblybiogra_rsls.htm or www.library.csi.cuny.edu/dept/history/lavender/386/ nellie.html.

▶ Exercise 25

Apply your imagination to the situation you identified in the previous exercise, using one of the techniques discussed in Step 3. In other words, create a mental picture, produce relevant examples, create a realistic scenario, or construct a new viewpoint.

▶ Exercise 26

While reading an essay, you encounter this statement: "Each individual creates his or her own morality. The moment a person decides that a behavior is acceptable, it becomes acceptable for that person and no one else has any business criticizing the behavior." On a separate sheet of paper, create several realistic scenarios that could help you decide whether this viewpoint is reasonable. Then decide what those scenarios suggest about the viewpoint.

Step 4: Check sources

Did you hear about the high school student from India who proved Albert Einstein wrong and is being considered for a Nobel prize in physics? Have you read about the recently discovered 1895 eighth-grade examination proving that students back then were far superior academically to today's students? Both these stories, and many others that may be waiting right now in your e-mail box, are *false rumors* or *hoaxes*. They often come to you from people you know, sometimes from individuals who are usually alert but from time to time fail to check before passing a story on.

Whenever you encounter an interesting story or a startling claim, try to determine where it came from. If you encounter it in your reading, look for source citations such as footnotes or endnotes. In magazines and newspapers the sources are often mentioned in the article itself. Be wary when no sources are mentioned or they are identified only as "knowledgeable people" or "individuals who prefer to remain anonymous."

If people you know tell you the story or make the claim, ask where they encountered it. If they read it somewhere, ask where; if they heard it from someone, ask whom. Don't be surprised if they can't say—they may have assumed it was true and never checked it.

If the source is provided, check it. If no source is given, check with an appropriate source. For example, check a health claim with a medical organization and a story about pending federal legislation with your congressional representative's office. The following websites are especially helpful for checking rumors and hoaxes:

http://hoaxbusters.ciac.org/HBOtherHoaxPages.html

http://urbanlegends.miningco.com/culture/urbanlegends/library/
blhoax.htm?pid=2733&cob=home

www.truthorfiction.com/

⏩ Exercise 27

Visit and explore the three websites mentioned above—that is, Hoaxbusters, Urban Legends, and Truth or Fiction. Explain below which you find most helpful and why.

_____

_____

_____

Habits for individuality

At the beginning of this chapter, we noted that we are not born with individuality but, instead, with the potential to develop it. We then discussed a number of ways for you to develop that potential—by acknowledging how other people influence you, by adopting positive and constructive attitudes, and by recognizing and resisting manipulation.

This section explains an additional way to develop your individuality—by cultivating the habits associated with critical thinking, the most important of which are these:

Be wary of first impressions

You're at a party and notice several people standing near you. One of them says, "Betty, meet George." You're shocked. You've met this guy before. His name isn't George, you think. It's Ed. Later, you seek out the person who made the introduction and ask him if he made a mistake. He assures you he didn't.

As the evening wears on, you hear other people saying "George" this and "George" that. You reflect on the dozens, hundreds of times you've called him Ed. Apparently he was too polite to correct you. Your face flushes with embarrassment at the thought. "How could I have been so dumb?" you say over and over to yourself.

But the problem is not a lack of intelligence—it is the bad habit of relying on first impressions and closing your mind to later perceptions. And this habit has more serious consequences than mispronouncing a name. It can increase your vulnerability to manipulation and the pressure to conform.

The solution to this problem is not to take first impressions for granted. Instead, remain open to subsequent impressions and decide whether they confirm or disconfirm your first impressions.

Be honest with yourself

One of the most memorable lines in philosophy is the directive "Know thyself." The key to following this wise advice is to be completely honest with yourself. This is not as easy as it sounds. It means facing a number of unpleasant truths, notably the following:

Much that we blame on others is really our own fault.

When we deny our mistakes, we compound them.

Others can usually see our faults better than we can.

Most of us tend to be too concerned about our rights and not concerned enough about our responsibilities.

Much that we think we know, we really only guess or assume.

The first step in self-improvement is admitting the need for it.

Fight confusion

Like everyone else, critical thinkers are sometimes confused. What sets critical thinkers apart is that they respond actively to confusion. For example, if the meaning of a sentence escapes them, instead of just accepting confusion, they consider a number of *possible* meanings and then choose the most likely one. And if a question arises and they don't know the answer, they look in a reference book or check with an authority to find it.

How might you apply this approach? Suppose you are somewhat puzzled by this proverb: "The girl who can't dance says the band can't play." You might wonder if the reference here is just to dancing or to other situations as well. Just how broad is its meaning? Then you would consider how the proverb might apply to other situations, such as a small boy having trouble catching a ball and blaming the thrower or a student having trouble with a course and blaming the teacher. Finally, you would conclude that the proverb refers to any situation in which people tend to blame others for their own shortcomings.

Produce many ideas

Many people are idea-poor. When confronted by a challenge, they embrace the first response that pops into their minds, often one that they have seen in print or heard on television. With that approach, the odds of their producing insightful ideas are slender.

Consider this example. When the price of a postage stamp was increased by three cents, people with a supply of the older stamps had to combine them with three-cent stamps to make the correct postage. The lines at post offices in some areas were unusually long, and the demand for three-cent stamps quickly exceeded the supply. One reason was that some people bought many more stamps than they needed. For example, people who needed ten three-cent stamps bought fifty or 100. (Perhaps they believed the stamps would increase in value.)

It got even sillier. One man entering a post office saw the sign "Sorry, we're temporarily out of three-cent stamps." He grumbled in displeasure and said as he walked away, "I've driven to four post offices and they're all out of stamps. Now I've got to try a fifth." Apparently he never considered other options. He could have walked up to the window, bought some four-cent stamps—plenty were available—and mailed his letters.

To avoid such embarrassing mistakes, produce lots of ideas before embracing any one. Extend your effort to identify possibilities. A helpful technique is *springboarding*. Here's how it works: Think of an idea and add to it right away. Resist the urge to dwell on details. Don't worry about writing complete sentences; a word or short phrase will do. Use one idea to propel you to others. To keep the process going, end each item in your list with the word *and*.

Let's say that the subject you are addressing is students' attitudes in class. Your list of ideas might be as shown in the box on this page. The cue questions are italicized. Note how asking questions cues you to continue springboarding.

Here is an additional tip: Be open to ideas at all times. You may find that insights occur to you when you don't expect them—while you shower, walk from class to class, or fall asleep at night. Perhaps you said to yourself on some of these occasions, "I've got to remember this idea later," and found later that you had forgotten it.

What Attitudes?
disinterest in class and hostility to the teacher and . . .

Are There More?
disapproval of students who speak and uncooperativeness in class discussion and disrespect for other students and . . .

How Are Attitudes Revealed?
smirking and whispering while others are talking and arriving late for class and making rude remarks and doing unrelated things like cleaning nails and . . .

Why Do Students Do These Things?
to maintain a "tough" image and to hide fear of failing and to make teachers uncomfortable and . . .

What Are Some Favorable Attitudes?
cooperativeness and willingness to listen to others' viewpoints and patience when the discussion gets complex and . . .

How Are These Attitudes Revealed?
looking at the person speaking and waiting for her to finish before you speak and refraining from side discussions and emphasizing the positive and . . .

This list could be continued. You could think about how some students develop positive attitudes and others develop negative ones. Or you might explore how teachers can effectively deal with students who have negative attitudes.

Keep a pen and paper handy to record ideas as they come to you. Once you start doing so, chances are you'll be rewarded with many more ideas.

Acknowledge complexity

In controversial issues the truth is often complex. Unfortunately, those are the very issues in which we are tempted to oversimplify. For example, when the issue of the integrity of politicians arises, we may immediately think "They're all crooks and hypocrites." Actually, this thought is inaccurate and irresponsible. Some politicians may be dishonest and hypocritical but many, arguably most, aren't. Moreover, the challenge of balancing the needs of different constituencies may create the appearance of dishonesty where it does not exist. Fairness demands that each politician be judged individually and on the basis of careful analysis, not preconceived notions.

Before you judge any issue, consider whether it may be more complex than it appears. And if it is, make your judgment reflect that complexity.

Look for connections among subjects

Over the centuries, educators found it convenient to divide human knowledge into various subject areas and to assign each to a separate academic department. There are English departments, history departments, chemistry departments, and so on. An unfortunate and unintended consequence of such division is the tendency to consider each subject area as totally unrelated to other subject areas.

In reality, the principles, concepts, and strategies learned in one subject often apply to other subjects as well. Moreover, most serious problems touch many subject areas. AIDS, for example, creates not only medical challenges but psychological, legal, and moral challenges as well. The more open you are to the relationships that exist among subjects, the more you will be rewarded with new insights.

Consider other viewpoints

To many people, intellectual independence means ignoring other people's views. This perspective hinders learning. Life is too short for learning solely through your limited experiences. By adding other people's ideas and experiences to your own, you will be able to broaden and deepen your knowledge, and do so more quickly than you would otherwise. In the process you will often gain valuable insights.

Could openness to other people's viewpoints cause you to lose your intellectual independence? Yes, but only if you accept their views uncritically. As long as you test their ideas before accepting them, you will have nothing to fear.

The contribution of psychologist Carol Tavris to our understanding of anger provides a good example of openness to all views PLUS critical thinking. She began her work by considering the widespread belief that expressing anger openly makes us feel less angry. But she didn't stop there. She also considered dissenting views and thought critically about all her findings. Ultimately, she decided that the widespread belief was wrong—that expressing our anger tends to reinforce and even intensify it. Tavris presented this view in her insightful book, *Anger: The Misunderstood Emotion.*

Base your judgments on evidence

What made Carol Tavris's book on anger so valuable was not that her judgment was original but that she supported it with an impressive amount of persuasive evidence based on scientific research. That is not surprising—the real measure of any viewpoint is how well it fits reality and that is determined by the amount and the quality of the evidence.

Unfortunately, many people ignore the need for evidence. They typically form judgments first and seek support for them later. The support they end up with is often nothing more than wishful thinking or foolish excuses. For example, some people say, "I smoke because science hasn't conclusively proved that it is harmful," "I don't use sunscreen because I'm not susceptible to skin cancer," or "I don't wear seatbelts because I don't want to be trapped in case I get in an accident." All three statements conveniently ignore the considerable evidence supporting the *opposite* view.

We humans are a proud species. Once we form a judgment, even a careless one, we are reluctant to change it because doing so means admitting a mistake. The best way to prevent pride from blocking insight is to keep your judgment tentative until you have examined the evidence.

▨ Exercise 28

Using the approaches you learned in this and previous chapters, evaluate each of the following passages. In the space provided state and briefly support your conclusion.

"I'm fascinated with the future because the future is where we're going to spend the rest of our lives."

_____

_____

_____

_____

⬗ Exercise 28 (cont.)

A television commercial for a used car sales agency says, "We'll cosign your loan even if you've had a bankruptcy. That's because we take the trouble to hand-pick and inspect these cars before you even see them. . . . We guarantee financing because we only sell quality cars."

_____

_____

_____

_____

A guest on a self-help radio program says, "In my counseling practice, I advise my clients to replace all their negative thoughts with positive ones. In other words, if they think 'I'm impatient,' they should say, 'No, I'm patient.' 'I'm clumsy' becomes 'I'm graceful,' and 'I'm a poor athlete' becomes 'I'm an excellent athlete.' I tell them that whatever they believe themselves to be, they will be."

_____

_____

_____

_____

⬗ Exercise 29

When Budweiser Dry beer was introduced, a series of television commercials appeared on the theme "Why ask why? Try Bud Dry." The structure of the ad was to raise a few questions, such as "The Mona Lisa has no eyebrows. Why?" and "Chickens have no lips. Why?" and then to recite the slogan, "Why ask why? Try Bud Dry." Was this advertisement manipulative? If so, in what way? What harmful effect, if any, might it have had?

_____

_____

_____

_____

⏩ Exercise 30

On a separate sheet of paper express a *tentative* opinion about each of the following issues. Then ask pertinent questions about what you have written, apply the techniques of imagination, and check the sources of your information. If your information is inadequate, do further research on the Internet or in the library. Finally, revise your view, as necessary, to make it reasonable.

Can animals think?

Should gambling be legalized?

Should teachers be allowed to spank elementary school children who misbehave in school?

Do smokers tend to discount the evidence that smoking can kill them?

Should the government assume control of the Internet, deciding who can have access and under what conditions?

Is it wrong to criticize another person's view of a controversial issue?

Is it acceptable to subject animals to painful experiments in order to find cures for diseases?

Is it possible for atheists to be as moral as religious believers?

☑ quiz

Write your answers on a separate sheet of paper.

1. What is the first step in becoming an individual as explained in this chapter?

2. Most of us were, and still are, vulnerable to the influences of other people. True or false? Explain your answer.

3. What is an "attitude"?

4. The chapter uses the term "culture war". Define that term and identify the parties to the conflict.

5. State the four "empowering attitudes" discussed in the chapter.

6. How does manipulation differ from other influences?

7. Name two forms of manipulation and explain why we should resist them.

8. Identify the steps in the strategy suggested for resisting manipulation.

9. List three habits for individuality and explain why each is important.

Answers to this quiz may be found at http://college.hmco.com.

CHAPTER **4**

Evaluating Arguments

IN THIS CHAPTER:

What is an argument?
An argument is the presentation of a point of view in the hope of persuading others.

Conducting library research
These tips will help you find information in the library.

Conducting Internet research
These tips will help you find information on the Internet.

Conducting an interview
These tips will help you acquire information in meetings with knowledgeable people.

Avoiding plagiarism
Plagiarism is passing off other people's ideas or words as one's own. It both steals and deceives.

Revisiting evidence
This expanded discussion of evidence will help you ask the right questions when you analyze arguments.

Evaluating complex arguments
This section reveals how conducting research fits into the thinking strategy discussed in Chapter One.

A caution about bias
In evaluating an argument, the greatest obstacle to critical thinking is your own bias.

87

What is an argument?

The word *argument* is sometimes used in the sense of "quarrel"—that is, a dispute characterized by angry exchanges. We will use the term differently, to mean *the statement of a point of view and the evidence that supports it in a way intended to be persuasive to other people.* Candidates for political office argue when they present their positions on issues. Lawyers argue when they try cases in court. Scholars in various academic fields argue when they offer new theories or interpretations. Students argue when they take a position on an issue in class discussion or answer an essay question that calls for judgment.

An argument expresses a "line of reasoning," which may be thought of as a kind of equation, such as *a* plus *b* equals *c*. Whether the argument is sound or unsound depends on what is actually said in the equation. "Twenty plus seventy equals ninety" is sound. On the other hand, "Thirteen plus fourteen equals thirty" is unsound. So is "Roses are red; Irish setters are red; therefore, Irish setters are roses."

Arguments can vary in length from a single sentence to a brief essay or even to a 100,000-word book. The simplest kinds of arguments consist of stating what we think and why we think it. More complex arguments contain a network of assertions or claims, together with supporting data. Chapter One discussed simple arguments; this chapter will focus on complex arguments.

Logic offers numerous rules for deciding whether an argument is sound. Those rules are beyond the scope of this book. We will continue to focus on the most fundamental test—whether the argument can be demonstrated to be more reasonable than competing arguments. And we will continue to use the comprehensive thinking strategy presented in Chapter One. However, in this chapter that strategy is modified to reflect the special challenge presented by complex arguments. This modification will enable you to become as proficient in analyzing those arguments as you have become in analyzing simple ones. Here is a comparison of the earlier strategy and the new one:

ORIGINAL STRATEGY (CHAPTER ONE)	**REVISED STRATEGY**
Step 1: Identify facts and opinions	Step 1: Identify facts and opinions
Step 2: Check the facts and test the opinion(s)	Step 2: Check the facts and test the opinions
Step 3: Evaluate the evidence	Step 3: Conduct research
Step 4: Make your judgment	Step 4: Evaluate the evidence
	Step 5: Make your judgment

We will return to the revised strategy later in the chapter, after discussing library and Internet research and expanding our treatment of evidence. Let's begin with research.

Conducting library research

Research is merely a matter of finding information, and all that is necessary to do that, in any given situation, is to identify relevant sources of information and then consult them. Following are the most basic information sources. The most important library source is the professional staff that works there. Ask your campus librarian to help you identify the sources listed below and answer any other research questions.

For a broad overview of a subject: an encyclopedia. An encyclopedia is a compendium of information about a wide variety of topics and is therefore a good starting point for research. Each article is written by a person or persons with specific knowledge of that subject.

For statistical data and miscellaneous facts: an almanac. The best known almanacs include *The World Almanac* and *Information Please Almanac*.

For newspaper reports: The *New York Times Index*. This index is the standard newspaper index for the United States. It covers all stories that appeared in that newspaper from 1851 to the present.

▶ Good Thinking!

The Melvil Dewey Story

Imagine how difficult it would be to use a library if there were no system for shelving the books. If you wanted a particular book, you'd have no idea how to find it. It might be on the top shelf of aisle one, the bottom shelf of aisle forty, or anywhere in between. The larger the library, the more difficult it would be to use. A large university library would be virtually *impossible* to use.

The situation was never that bad, but up until 1876 the system in use was inflexible and cumbersome. Each book had a designated place on the library shelves. A book on astronomy might be between a book on woodworking and another on medieval architecture. Then Melvil Dewey, a student assistant in the Amherst College library, had the creative idea that brought him fame and the appreciation of library users everywhere.

Dewey's creative idea was to invent a new shelving system, which came to be known as the Dewey Decimal System. When he left Amherst, he installed the system in Columbia University and then in the New York State Public Library.

The Dewey Decimal System has ten main divisions: 000 is Computers, Information, and General Reference; 100, Philosophy and Psychology; 200, Religion; 300, Social Sciences; 400, Language; 500, Science; 600, Technology; 700, Arts and Recreation; 800, Literature; 900 History and Geography. Each division has a series of subdivisions. Dewey's system makes it possible to manage—and to use—any library more flexibly and efficiently. Today it is used in more than 135 countries and has been translated into more than thirty languages. It is also proving useful in classifying Internet resources.

Dewey's devotion to improving things also led to other achievements. He is credited with establishing the first library school, reforming library standards, and (with others) founding the American Library Association. In addition, he was a pioneer in creating job opportunities for women.

For more information on Melvil Dewey, see www.homeschoollearning.com/hsc/unit_09-10-01.html, or www.oclc.org/dewey/resources/biography/.

For general magazines and journals: *Reader's Guide to Periodical Literature.* The *Reader's Guide* is an index of articles published in popular magazines.

For specialized periodicals: an appropriate index. Specialized indexes provide information on articles in scholarly journals comparable to the information *Reader's Guide* provides about popular articles.

For government publications: a state or federal monthly catalog. State and federal governments publish more documents than any other publishing source.

For abstracts of scholarly works: an appropriate data base or abstract service. These sources offer summaries of scholarly articles in various fields.

For library holdings: your library's computer catalog. This source is your key to the books, tapes, monographs, and other materials available in your library. If you are looking for a specific title that is not available in your library, your librarian will usually be able to obtain it from another library. You can also visit your college's official website.

 Exercise 31

To use many of the information sources listed above you'll need to ask your campus librarian. Carry out that direction for each of the sources and record your librarian's response.

_____

_____

_____

_____

_____

Conducting Internet research

Despite its brief history, the Internet has already become a major research venue, largely because it can be accessed without leaving home. Many traditional library resources are also available online. Following are two tips for efficient Internet research:

Use a search engine

The name "search engine" conjures up the image of a large machine, but a more appropriate image might be that of a person who assists you in finding information. A search engine is really a "research assistant." (We'll call this assistant "it" because it is genderless.) You tell it your thoughts by writing in a blank box, hit "search," and it searches the World Wide Web of information for you and, in the blink of an eye, provides a list of locations where you can find what you are looking for.

This assistant can do everything . . . except read your mind. It will look for exactly what you tell it, nothing more or less. Therefore you must choose your terms with care and revise them if you don't get the information you want.

There are many search engines and even metasearch engines, which search other search engines. For a clear and thorough explanation of the difference and some helpful suggestions, visit this University of California at Berkeley website: www.lib.berkeley.edu/TeachingLib/Guides/Internet/MetaSearch.html.

The main search engine recommended at that site is www.google.com. By making Google your personal assistant, you will ensure that your Internet searches are quick and effective.

Develop a resource list

The first dozen or so times you do Internet research, you will probably have to go to Google, type in the subject, and sample the results before you find helpful sites. In time, this approach will produce a resource list for specific subjects. Following is a brief list of helpful websites to get you started:

For reference materials, including dictionaries, encyclopedias, and more:
www.bartleby.com/reference
www.infoplease.com

For news:
www.foxnews.com
www.ap.org
www.cnn.com

For informed opinion:
www.townhall.com (Click on "columnists" and then on any of the featured columns or on any person's name.)
www.jewishworldreview.com (Click on any of the names in the Insight column toward the bottom of the home page.)
www.prospect.org
www.demsonline.net (click on "links")
www.frontpagemag.com
www.blueagle.com (This site lists 700 columnists, many cartoonists, and links to political websites.)

For quotations:
www.toinspire.com

For legal information:
www.legalengine.com
www.law.com
www.nolo.com

For health and medicine:
www.nih.gov
www.medlineplus.gov

For checking the quality/credibility of a website: One problem in doing research on the Internet is that, unlike newspapers, magazines, and books, it is not subject to editorial scrutiny. Anyone can publish anything, and there is a greater risk of receiving erroneous information. The following resources can help minimize that risk:

http://infodome.sdsu.edu/research/evaluate/samples.shtml

www.lib.duke.edu/libguide/evaluating_web.htm

www2.widener.edu/Wolfgram-Memorial-Library/webeval/eval1198/index.htm (This site offers an excellent PowerPoint presentation prepared by Jan Alexander and Marsha Ann Tate of Widener University.)

www.sosig.ac.uk/desire/internet-detective.html (This site offers an unusually comprehensive—two-hour long—tutorial on evaluating Internet resources.)

A helpful tip: Some Internet searches will take you to sites that seem objective but really serve to sell you products and services. Such sites end in ".com" which stands for "commercial." (Note: The ending ".com" does not *necessarily* signify a lack of objectivity.) You can eliminate commercial websites from your Google searches by adding at the end of your search term the minus sign followed (without a space) by ".com." For example, if your search term were "vitamin therapy" you would type "vitamin therapy-.com" without using the quotation marks.

▨▶ Exercise 32

Visit the Internet Public Library (IPL) at www.ipl.org/ and examine the resources available there. Compare this information with the list of online resources mentioned by your librarian in Exercise 31. Report the results of your investigation in the space provided below.

_____

_____

_____

_____

_____

Exercise 33

This exercise is designed to help you become familiar with Google. Go to the Google website—www.google.com—and click, in turn, on each of the blue words on the homepage. As you read each of the pages that appear, click on key words to learn more about Google's offerings. List below the features you find most useful.

_____

_____

_____

_____

_____

 Exercise 34

Go to the Google homepage again. In the search box, type the words *free online encyclopedia* and then click the search button. Then click on each of the first ten search results (more, if you wish) and decide which ones you find most helpful. Repeat this procedure with the phrases *free online almanac* and *government publications*. Record your decisions below and add the websites to your personal resource list.

_____

_____

_____

_____

_____

_____

Conducting an interview

Your research needn't be limited to the library and the Internet. A number of instructors at your college may have expertise on your topic. If you decide to interview one or more of them, call to make an appointment and state what you want to interview them about and how long you will need. Here are some tips for conducting the interview.

1. Arrive on time and don't overstay your welcome.

2. Ask for permission to tape the interview so the instructor will not have to wait while you take notes.

3. Avoid asking questions calling for a "yes" or "no" answer. Instead, ask "What do you think about . . . ?" and "What is the basis for your thinking . . . ?"

4. Pay attention to the instructor's answers and ask follow-up questions where appropriate.

On the rare occasions when you can't find appropriate people with expertise at your college, use your ingenuity. For a medical issue, call the state public health department or the county medical association. The telephone directory will list the numbers of these agencies. Ask to be referred to an expert in your area.

Avoiding plagiarism*

Once ideas are put into words and published, they become "intellectual property," and the author has the same rights over them as he or she has over a material possession such as a house or a car. The only real difference is that intellectual property is purchased with mental effort rather than money. Anyone who has ever wracked his or her brain trying to solve a problem or trying to put an idea into clear and meaningful words can appreciate how difficult mental effort can be.

Plagiarism is passing off other people's ideas or words as one's own. It is doubly offensive in that it both steals and deceives. In the academic world, plagiarism is considered an ethical violation and is punished by a failing grade for a paper or a course, or even by dismissal from the institution. Outside the academy, it is a crime that can be prosecuted if the person to whom the ideas and words belong wishes to bring charges.

Some cases of plagiarism are attributable to intentional dishonesty, others to carelessness. But many, perhaps most, are due to misunderstanding. The instructions "Base your paper on research rather than on your own unfounded opinions" and "Don't present other people's ideas as your own" seem contradictory and may confuse students, especially if no clarification is offered. Fortunately, there is a way to honor both instructions and, in the process, to avoid plagiarism.

Step 1: When you are researching a topic, keep your sources' ideas separate from your own. Begin by keeping a record of each source of information you consult. For an Internet source, record the website address, the author and title of the item, and the date you visited the site. For a book, record the author, title, place of publication, publisher, and date of

---

* This section is used with permission. Copyright © 2002 by MindPower, Inc.

publication. For a magazine or journal article, record the author, title, the name of the publication, and its date of issue. For a TV or radio broadcast, record the program title, station, and date of transmission.

Step 2: As you read each source, note the ideas you want to refer to in your writing. If the author's words are unusually clear and concise, copy them *exactly* and put quotation marks around them. Otherwise, paraphrase—that is, restate the author's ideas in your words. Write down the number(s) of the page on which the author's passage appears.

If the author's idea triggers a response in your mind—such as a question, a connection between this idea and something else you've read, or an experience of your own that supports or challenges what the author says—write it down and put brackets (not parentheses) around it so that you will be able to identify it as your own when you review your notes. Here is a sample research record illustrating these two steps:

> Adler, Mortimer J. *The Great Ideas: A Lexicon of Western Thought* (New York: Macmillan Publishing Co., 1992) Says that throughout the ages, from ancient Greece, philosophers have argued about whether various ideas are true. Says it's remarkable that most renowned thinkers have agreed about what truth is—"a correspondence between thought and reality." 867 Also says that Freud saw this as the *scientific* view of truth. Quotes Freud: "This correspondence with the real external world we call truth. It is the aim of scientific work, even when the practical value of that work does not interest us." 869 [I say true statements fit the facts; false statements do not.]

Whenever you look back on this record, even a year from now, you will be able to tell at a glance which ideas and words are the author's and which are yours. The first three sentences are, with the exception of the directly quoted part, *paraphrases* of the author's ideas. The fourth is a direct quotation. The final sentence, in brackets, is your own idea.

Step 3: When you compose your paper, work borrowed ideas and words into your writing by judicious use of quoting and paraphrasing. In addition, give credit to the various authors. Your goal here is to eliminate all doubt about which ideas and words belong to whom. In formal presentations, this crediting is done in footnotes; in informal ones, it is done simply by mentioning the author's name.

Here is an example of how source material can be worked into a composition. The first paragraph contains the quoted and paraphrased material from Mortimer Adler. (You would insert a footnote or endnote number at the end of that paragraph and the note would provide the necessary citation.) The second paragraph adds *your own original commentary* on the Adler material.

> Mortimer J. Adler explains that throughout the ages, from the time of the ancient Greeks, philosophers have argued about

whether various ideas are true. But to Adler the remarkable thing is that, even as they argued, most renowned thinkers have agreed about what truth is. They saw it as "a correspondence between thought and reality." Adler points out that Sigmund Freud believed this was also the scientific view of truth. He quotes Freud as follows: "This correspondence with the real external world we call truth. It is the aim of scientific work, even when the practical value of that work does not interest us."

This correspondence view of truth is consistent with the common sense rule that a statement is true if it fits the facts and false if it does not. For example, the statement "the twin towers of New York's World Trade Center were destroyed on September 11, 2002" is false because they were destroyed the previous year. I may sincerely believe that it is true, but my believing in no way affects the truth of the matter. In much the same way, if an innocent man is convicted of a crime, neither the court's decision nor the world's acceptance of it will make him any less innocent. We may be free to think what we wish, but our thinking can't change reality.

Revisiting evidence

Chapter One defined *evidence* as reliable information offered in support of an opinion. In that chapter, we noted that there are various kinds of evidence, but we focused on just one—the *reasons* people offer for thinking and acting as they do. The term *reasons* can also be used in a broader, more general way to cover *all* forms of evidence. There is nothing wrong in using the term that way. However, you will find it helpful to become familiar with the more *specific* terms, as well. Doing so will enable you to ask pertinent questions whenever you analyze arguments. Following are eight other kinds of evidence, together with the appropriate questions to ask about each:

Anecdotes and cases-in-point

These include brief examples as well as illustrations and more extended narratives of people's experiences and observations. They are often vivid and dramatic and therefore can be very persuasive. Suppose someone says, "Telephone solicitors can be very rude" and proceeds to describe a recent experience she had with a caller. The example "backs up" her assertion. Of course, if the claim were more sweeping, such as "Most telephone solicitors are rude," more than a single example would be needed. The person making the claim would be challenged to show that the rudeness she encountered was typical of telephone solicitors.

To test anecdotes and cases-in point, ask: *Is the author's presentation of the anecdote or case faithful to the facts? If so, are the experiences described typical or untypical? How plausible are they? How might I verify them?*

Published reports

Published reports are found in newspapers, broadcasts, books, and magazines and on the Internet. This kind of evidence is very common but not always reliable. There are some careless and dishonorable reporters who allow their biases to influence their reporting. And even conscientious reporters can make mistakes. The chance for error is especially great when the information is acquired in haste or from second- or third-hand accounts. Never assume that a report is accurate just because it appears in print or is broadcast.

To test a published report, ask: *What information sources, if any, are cited in the report?* If sources are cited, they can often be checked quite easily, especially if they have a website. (A trip to Google will reveal that.) Remember, though, that verifying that the source did say what was claimed does not establish the source's accuracy.

Eyewitness testimony

Eyewitness testimony is a report of what someone observed firsthand. Such testimony is popularly regarded as highly reliable. After all, there is something very persuasive about a seemingly honest person who says, "I saw it happen" and goes on to provide the details of who, how, and where. However, research has shown that eyewitness testimony is sometimes false. Perception can be blinded by preconceived notions and the memory of an earlier event can be corrupted by subsequent events.

To test eyewitness testimony, ask: *Does the person have anything to gain by misrepresenting the facts? Were the conditions favorable to observation— for example, did the event occur in the daytime or at night, in good weather or bad (snow, rain, or fog)? Did the event occur slowly or quickly? Was it expected or unexpected? Was the person in a state of mind conducive to accurate observation? Sober or drunk? Tired or well rested? Calm or emotional (for example, fearful)? Could the person's memory have been confused by something that occurred after the event but before the testimony was given?*

Expert testimony

This kind of testimony has the advantage of being informed by extensive knowledge of the subject and understanding of what is typical in most cases. Such testimony is therefore highly reliable. However, experts often disagree in their assessments. Even when they agree they can be mistaken, so this generally reliable testimony cannot be taken at face value.

To test expert testimony, ask: *Does the person have specific expertise in the subject in question?* (It is not uncommon these days for experts to offer opinions far outside their areas of expertise.) *Does the expert's view represent the majority or minority view among experts in the field? In other words, do other experts agree with the person in question?*

▶ Good Thinking!

The Story of Walter Reed

Yellow fever is believed to have been brought to Central America from Africa on slave ships in the late sixteenth century. No fewer than ninety epidemics hit the United States between then and 1900, one in 1793 killing 10 percent of the population of Philadelphia. Napoleon reportedly sold the Louisiana Territory to the United States because the disease claimed 90 percent of the forces he had stationed there.

Walter Reed had graduated from the University of Virginia medical program at age 17, the youngest graduate in the program's history. Reed served as an Army surgeon before returning to Maryland in 1890 to study bacteriology and pathology. This preparation proved crucial when he was sent to Cuba to do research on yellow fever.

The disease began with chills and a headache, then progressed to severe pain, high fever, and vomiting. Next came jaundice, followed in extreme cases by internal bleeding and death. Medical experts thought the cause was bacterial. Reed doubted that because the disease appeared neither contagious nor airborne. A person in one house would fall victim while other family members and neighbors were spared. Reed chose instead to pursue an older, discredited idea that insects were transmitting the disease.

Reed was challenged to disprove the bacteria theory and to prove the insect theory, so he devised an ingenious experiment. He had one group of Army volunteers sleep on the clothing and beds of yellow fever patients in a screened room (to keep mosquitoes out). No one in this group became infected. Meanwhile, he kept another group completely apart from infected people and their belongings. But this group he exposed to mosquitoes that had been in the rooms of infected people. These volunteers became infected.

Having proved how yellow fever was transmitted, Reed had the Army install mosquito nets and wipe out mosquito breeding grounds in and around Havana. These efforts were so successful in ending the scourge that the same approach was used in Panama, thus removing a major obstacle to the construction of the Panama Canal.

Walter Reed was awarded the Congressional Medal of Honor for his contribution to the eradication of yellow fever. He also became the first physician to be elected to the Hall of Fame of Great Americans at New York University. The Walter Reed Army Medical Center in Washington DC is named after him.

For more information on Walter Reed, see www.wramc.amedd.army.mil/welcome/history/index1.htm.

Experiments

One kind of experiment is the kind performed under controlled circumstances, such as in a laboratory. Another kind is the field experiment, in which observation is conducted in natural surroundings. For example, one might observe a group of children at play, participants at a political convention, or Amish farmers raising a barn. For the results of the observation to be reliable, the observer must not have influenced the behavior of the group. Also, the period of observation must have been of reasonable duration.

To test a laboratory experiment, ask: *Have the findings of the experiment been confirmed by other, independent researchers?* To test a field experiment, ask: *Did the presence of the investigator influence the outcome?*

Statistical studies

Statistics usually refers to quantitative information obtained about every individual in a group or category. Examples of statistics are the percentage of deaths caused by drunken driving, the comparative college admissions scores of various racial and ethnic groups, and the voting records of members of Congress. If the statistical sources are reputable, the statistics will generally be trustworthy. But it is prudent to check that they are quoted accurately.

To test statistical evidence, ask: *Is the source of the data reliable? How long ago were the statistics compiled? Have conditions changed since then?*

Surveys

This type of information is a subdivision of statistics. However, it is obtained in a special way—by a sampling of the group. The sample may be random or systematic (for example, every fiftieth name in the phone book). It may also be done in person, by telephone, or by mail. A sample can be reliable even though a very small number of individuals were contacted, but only if certain conditions were met. All members of the group must have had an equal chance of being contacted. Also, the questions must have been clear, unambiguous, and unbiased. Keep in mind that the way survey questions are phrased can influence the responses.

To test a survey, ask: *Was the sample representative of the larger group? Were the questions clear and objective? For mail surveys, did too few people respond for the survey results to be trusted?*

Research reviews

Research reviews examine the general body of research information on a topic. It is not uncommon for such a review to cover dozens, even hundreds, of independent research studies. A research review is a highly reliable form of evidence if it covers all significant research studies and is free of bias.

To test a research review, ask: *Were any important studies omitted?*

Evaluating complex arguments

We began this chapter by noting that, when evaluating complex arguments, we need to modify the comprehensive thinking strategy presented in Chapter One. The new strategy has five steps: (1) Identify facts and opinions, (2) Check the facts and test the opinions, (3) Conduct research, (4) Evaluate the evidence, and (5) Make your judgment. Now that we have completed our discussion of evidence and the techniques of research, we will examine each of these steps, expanding on what was noted in Chapter One and demonstrating how the new step fits in the overall strategy.

Step 1: Identify facts and opinions

Before separating facts and opinions in any argument, you should first have an accurate understanding of the argument. This is easy to achieve with a short essay, a letter to a newspaper editor, or a brief opinion column. But it is more difficult with longer, more complex works such as feature articles, book chapters, and entire books. The following approach will help ensure that your understanding is accurate:

Skim for the central opinion. Before reading a longer article or book, skim it, looking for the central opinion—that is, the view of the issue the author wishes his or her audience to accept. The central opinion is usually stated in or immediately after the introduction and is reinforced in the conclusion. (Note: Introductions and conclusions vary in length. In a full-length article, each may occupy two or more paragraphs; in a book, each may be assigned its own chapter.)

Read the article or book carefully. With the author's central opinion clearly in mind, read the article or book carefully. Take note of the evidence (factual information) offered in support of the central opinion— for example, anecdotes, published reports, expert testimony, experiments, statistical studies, or surveys. Also note important secondary opinions, such as the main opinions of the subsections of an article or the chapters of a book, as well as the evidence offered for them. Remember that any statement that is open to dispute should be considered an opinion, even if the author presents it as factual.

Knowing the basic relationships between the parts of an argument can help you identify opinions and supporting evidence more effectively.

"And" relationships signal that what follows adds to what preceded. For example, they may signal that more evidence is being offered to support an assertion. Words used for "and" relationships include *also, first (second,* and so on); *in addition, next, further, and, moreover, finally, lastly, besides,* and *another.*

"But" relationships signal that what follows contrasts with what preceded. What follows is usually an exception or qualification. Words used to signal "but" relationships include *however, nevertheless, yet, or, but, on the other hand,* and *in contrast.*

"Therefore" relationships signal that a conclusion follows from the preceding evidence. Words used to signal "therefore" relationships include *so, consequently, accordingly, thus, therefore,* and *it follows that.*

Some high school English teachers discourage students from using *and* or *but* to begin a sentence. But that prohibition is unreasonable. Even a quick scanning of enduring works of literature reveals that writers have long used these words to begin sentences. You should therefore feel free to do so in your writing.

One common pattern in argumentative writing is the "and/therefore" pattern. For example, a member of Congress may argue:

> "The economy is in a recession. . . . **And** history has demonstrated that a decrease in personal income tax is an economic stimulant. . . . **Therefore,** the President's proposal to cut taxes deserves the support of both political parties."

Another common pattern is the "but, therefore" pattern. For example, a professor may argue:

> "All students benefit from attending class regularly. . . . **But** many students lack the self-discipline to attend class regularly on their own. . . . **Therefore,** this college should adopt a compulsory attendance policy."

Longer articles and books typically include more elaborate patterns, such as _____, and _____, and _____, but _____, and _____, therefore _____. (The material represented by each line may comprise a sentence, a paragraph, or a chapter.)

Summarize. When you have finished reading the article or book and identifying the evidence offered in support of the main opinion, write a summary. An effective summary (1) is written, as much as possible, in your own words; (2) records only the major parts of the argument—that is, the main and secondary opinions and a brief notation of the evidence offered in support of them; and (3) accurately reflects what the author has said. If the author emphasizes or qualifies a point, make your summary reflect it. If you wish to add your own comments, put them in brackets. Then, when you look back at your summary, you can easily distinguish your ideas from the author's.

▶ Exercise 35

Apply the procedure in Step 1 to the following argument. (Note that specific directions are given after the article.)

A Day's Pay for a Day's Work

Every year during football or basketball season, some college in the country makes headlines when one of its athletes is suspended for violating his amateur status by receiving money. Self-righteous windbags around the country then rant on about the importance of protecting college athletics from professionalism and ensuring that athletes place education before sports. Not only is that view hypocritical, it's also absurd. The best thing that could happen to college athletics would be for the myth of amateurism to be exposed and the NCAA to abandon its regulation prohibiting pay for play.

To begin with, college athletes have only one reason for going to college—to get a chance to play professional sports. They couldn't care less about an education. Many of them can't read and write, so the courses they take are just warmed-over junior high school subjects. The idea that their education is going to better their position in life is a cruel deception on them. Few others besides athletes are foolish enough to buy such a notion.

Some people argue that if college athletes were paid for playing sports, they would be corrupted. Surely it wouldn't be any less corrupting than the present situation, in which they receive money under the table and in the process violate ethics and the law. And it would spare universities that are supposed to represent society's highest values the embarrassment and shame that accompany unfavorable newspaper headlines.

The only sensible course of action for the NCAA, and for that matter the Olympic Committee, to take is to discard the phony distinction between amateur and professional. Let colleges run their athletic programs as money-making ventures (as many of them now do, dishonestly). Allow them to recruit the best players they can without having to enroll them in academic programs. And permit the players to earn salaries and work full time at their sports. The players will be happier, the teams will perform better, and everyone's consciences will be a lot clearer.

State the controlling idea of the article:

_____

_____

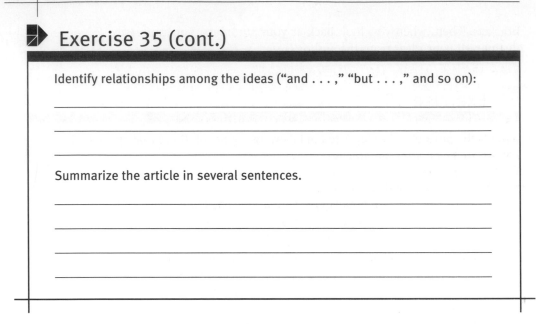

Exercise 35 (cont.)

Identify relationships among the ideas ("and . . . ," "but . . . ," and so on):

_____

_____

_____

Summarize the article in several sentences.

_____

_____

_____

_____

Step 2: Check the facts and test the opinions

This step is to be performed on your summary rather than on the entire article or book. Begin by checking the major statements of fact to verify that they are factual. For example, check to be sure descriptions of published reports, expert testimony, experiments, and statistical studies are accurate. This can often be done by consulting a few basic reference resources—an encyclopedia, an almanac, a newspaper archive, and/or a magazine index.

Next, test the author's main and secondary opinions, using one or more of the following approaches, each of which was explained in Chapter One:

- Consult everyday experience.
- Consider the opinion's likely consequences.
- Consider the implications.
- Think of exceptions.
- Think of counterexamples.
- Reverse the opinion.
- Look for relevant research.

As we saw in Chapter One, these approaches for checking facts and testing opinions are often sufficient to demonstrate the strengths and weaknesses of a brief, simple argument. However, more complex arguments usually require additional research. The next step in our strategy addresses that challenge.

Step 3: Conduct research

The main purpose of research is to identify opinions and interpretations of facts that differ from the ones in the argument you are analyzing. Such opinions and interpretations may not have made their way into the reference books yet. If you tend to agree with the argument, of course, you may be tempted to ignore competing views. To give in to this temptation is to think *uncritically* and deny yourself valuable insights.

Consider this example: You are examining the argument that slavery was invented by European explorers as a means of dominating Africans and Native Americans. The author supports this claim with hundreds of documented cases. You are so impressed with the case he makes that you are tempted to accept it uncritically. But you resist this temptation and look for challenges to the author's view.

As a result of your search, you find that a number of sources (for example, Thomas Sowell's *Race and Culture*) claim slavery is thousands of years old, has been practiced on every continent, and is still practiced in the African nations of Ghana, Sudan, and Mauritania. Moreover, these sources maintain that Western culture led the way in *abolishing* slavery. Whichever view of the issue you ultimately embrace, you will have benefited by refusing to accept the first argument you encountered.

You will already have consulted the basic resources listed in the sections of this chapter on conducting library and Internet research—that is, an encyclopedia, an almanac, a newspaper archive, and/or a general magazine index. Now consult the other sources—indexes to specialized periodicals, catalogs of government publications, databases, abstract services, and your library's computer catalog. Also search Google and/or the resources on your personal list. After identifying articles, books, and tapes that challenge the argument you are analyzing, obtain and examine them.

Step 4: Evaluate the evidence

At this point, you will have accumulated a sizeable amount of material and may need to sort out the points of agreement and disagreement. The best way to do so is to make a spreadsheet. Identify the authorities across the top of the page. Then list the various aspects of the issue down the left side of the page. Suppose you're investigating the issue "Should boxing be outlawed?" and you've consulted three individuals in addition to the author of the original argument. Here is how your spreadsheet might look.

Aspects of the Issue	Medical Doctor	Former Boxer	Sports Writer	Original Argument
Is boxing a sport?	No	Yes	Yes	No
Is the intention in boxing to injure the opponent?	Yes	Yes	No	Yes
Is boxing dangerous?	Yes	Yes	Yes	Yes
Can the risk of injury be overcome by training?	No	Yes	Yes	No
Can the risk of injury be overcome by protective gear?	No	No	Yes	No
Would outlawing boxing deny minorities a way out of poverty?	No	Yes	Yes	No

Note that on the boxing spreadsheet you can tell where the disagreements lie simply by looking next to each aspect of the issue. There is no disagreement on the danger of boxing, some disagreement on the aspect of intentional harm, and considerable disagreement on the other four aspects.

You may be wondering, "Why spend time breaking the issue into its various aspects when I will eventually have to form an overall view? Why not deal with the entire issue immediately?" The answer is that in a complex issue, there can be many insights, and they are seldom all found on one side. Even a person who is mistaken about the main aspects of the issue may be right about several lesser aspects. In cases where no single argument is completely sound, you will have to construct a better argument than *any* of the ones you have seen. In order to do this, you will have to be in command of all aspects.

After completing your spreadsheet, address the various aspects, one at a time. Review the evidence offered by each of the people you consulted for his or her opinion. (In most cases, the evidence will differ from person to person, both in quantity and quality.) Review, too, the evidence you accumulated in your own research. In light of all that evidence, decide whether the most reasonable answer to *each aspect* is yes, no, or partly yes and partly no.

Step 5: Make your judgment

Having assessed the various aspects of the issue, you will be ready to combine those assessments into a judgment of the overall issue. Here, for example, is a judgment you might make on the boxing issue. (Other judgments, of course, are possible.)

> Boxing is not properly classified as a sport because the contestants intend to injure each other. Thus, boxing is more dangerous than sport, in which injuries occur accidentally or because rules are broken. It's true that training and protective gear can reduce the threat to fighters but not eliminate it. For these reasons, I believe boxing should be outlawed. I admit that such action would deny members of minority groups one way of rising above poverty, but better ways can and should be created.

The advantage of using the five steps to reach a judgment is that they enable you to present and defend your position more effectively. You will be able to support each component part of your judgment with evidence and explain why your reasoning is more reasonable than the reasoning advanced by others.

A caution about bias

When you evaluate an argument, the greatest obstacle to critical thinking is not the complexity of the issue or the variety of viewpoints to be considered. It is, instead, your own biases. Here is a fairly typical example of how bias can stifle critical thinking.

Let's say you just read an article pointing out the deficiencies of homeschooling. Most parents who homeschool, the author says, are not trained teachers, and some have not even graduated from college. In addition, the author points out that even if the parent is a certified teacher, he or she is not likely to be skilled in art, music, *and* foreign languages, and will be unable to provide lab experience at home. Finally, the author argues that children who are homeschooled are deprived of opportunities for socializing with peers. Thus, in his view, they are woefully unprepared to relate to people of other religions and cultures.

Now suppose that you know little about homeschooling other than what you just read. Suppose, too, that you have graduated from public school, believe your experience there was positive, and therefore support traditional classroom education. Given these facts, your bias would be almost imperceptible—nothing more, really, than a slight leaning. Not enough to put you on alert, yet enough to cause you to accept the author's assessment at face value *and not bother to investigate the opposing viewpoint.*

If even a slight, subtle bias can keep you from thinking critically, it is not hard to imagine what a more substantial bias will do.

Incidentally, in the homeschooling issue (as in all controversial issues), there *is* another side to be considered. Creative homeschoolers have discovered ways to overcome or compensate for the lack of laboratories and other limitations. Homeschooled students often score as well as, and in some cases better than, public and private school graduates, and are as respectful of other people as are traditional graduates.

No one has yet formulated an anti-bias serum, so inoculation is not a choice. The best you can do is to recognize bias when it arises and develop ways of resisting it. Following are the most common types of bias and suggestions for dealing with them:

Bias toward what confirms your personal view. We all tend to be protective of our opinions. This is true whether we reason them out or borrow them from others. Whenever we encounter information that confirms one of our opinions, our automatic reaction is to accept it. Similarly, we tend to reject information that challenges our opinion. *Suggestion: Keep in mind that we all make mistakes from time to time. The sooner we find out we've made one, the better off we are. And the best way to find a mistake early is to be open to ideas that challenge our own.*

Bias toward familiar ideas. Suppose you walked into a cafeteria and had the choice of sitting with people you know or with strangers. Which would you choose? No doubt you would choose people you know because you'd feel more relaxed and comfortable with them. It's the same way with ideas. All of us tend to be more accepting of ideas we've heard before than we are of new ideas. *Suggestion: Remember that familiarity has little significance—the order in which we hear ideas and the frequency of our hearing them are matters of chance. The fact that we've heard something repeated a dozen times doesn't mean it is any more reliable than something we are hearing for the first time.*

Bias toward your likes and against your dislikes. We all have our personal preferences. There's nothing wrong with that. The problem arises only when we let them interfere with our judgment. If someone shares your taste in television programming, you may see her as a person of great wisdom and taste. In contrast, anyone who speaks critically of

your favorite programming may seem lacking in intelligence and perhaps intentional-
ly offensive. *Suggestion: Carry your preferences lightly. Remember that they may reflect
the influence from peers or popular culture more than they reflect your individuality.*

⏩ Exercise 36

Does TV violence harm viewers? Although this issue has been debated for
decades, it remains controversial today. Innumerable articles and books have
been written about it, and a sizeable body of research exists. Analyze this issue
using the five-step approach detailed in this chapter and present your findings on
a separate sheet of paper. Following are two opposing viewpoints on this issue to
get you started:

TV Violence Is Harmful
By Sarah Rothman

Television executives tend to adopt one of three responses to the issue of
whether TV violence is harmful. The first response is that TV violence can be no
more harmful than real life because it is a reflection of real life. The second
response is that TV violence can't possibly be harmful because millions of people watch it without picking up a gun and mowing down their neighbors. The
third response is that TV executives alone have the authority to decide program
content and the public has no say in the matter. This last view is sometimes
expressed, "If you don't like what we offer, change channels." None of these
positions is valid, as I will show.

To begin with, television violence is *not* a reflection of real life—it is a highly
compressed and sensationalized presentation of carefully selected incidents
from real life. For example, TV cops are typically confronted with several major
cases in each episode, such as a rape, a murder, and a bank robbery. Not only
do they solve them all, but the prosecutors take the cases to trial and obtain
convictions, *all within an hour,* including time for commercials and some
departmental romance. That's hardly realistic.

Secondly, it is silly to pretend that the only negative effect of TV violence that
is possible is mass murder. Less dramatic, more subtle harmful effects are not
only possible but evident, and they can occur without our being aware of them.
TV violence coarsens viewers and makes them more accepting of offensive
behavior in real life. The more they see fictional blood spilled, the less revolted
they are likely to be by the spilling of real blood. The more simulated rapes they
witness, the less outraged they are likely to be about genuine rape. The more
people they see beaten and tortured, the less likely they are to object to incidents of verbal abuse in everyday life. The more physical mayhem they witness
in dramatic shows, the more tolerant they are likely to be of verbal mayhem—
such as interrupting when others speak and shouting down those who disagree.

▶ Exercise 36 (cont.)

Once people become accepting of incivility in the people around them, they become prone to behaving rudely themselves. This is arguably why public displays of temper, including road rage, have become so common; why forgiveness and kindness are regarded as signs of weakness rather than strength of character; why loud confrontation has displaced reasoned discussion; and why fewer and fewer people feel guilty for their offensive behavior.

Finally, telling the public "If you don't like what we offer, change channels" adds insult to injury. It's very much like saying, "If the air quality in your city is poor, don't clean up the pollution—just stay indoors." In reality, the *airwaves* belong to all the people, just as the air does. The people therefore have a right to demand that the people licensed by the Federal Communications Commission to use the airwaves do so responsibly, with regard to the sentiments and safety of the public.

TV Violence Is Harmless

By Zbigniew Pietrowsky

They're at it again. The scapegoaters are back on the soapbox, condemning television programs and movies for the violent behavior reported in the daily news.

Here's a news flash for them. Violence was here long before television and movies existed. It's as old as human nature. The urge to hurt others comes from some dark place within the human heart, not from external bad example. The stories of "man's inhumanity to man" are as old as the urge they probe. History is filled with actual examples of warriors exchanging blows with rocks and clubs, slashing one another with knives and swords, shooting one another first with arrows and then with bullets, and dropping bombs on enemy cities.

With such realities a central theme of history, we should not be surprised that violence has always been a theme of fiction, the most modern form of which is the film or TV drama. Here as elsewhere, art is merely imitating life.

Watching a film or a TV drama is a powerful experience, to be sure. We become engrossed in the action. And in our imagination we may take part in it. When the villain strikes the hero, we "feel" the blow. When the hero strikes back, we strike with him. And when in the final reel, good triumphs, we enjoy a sense of relief, of mission accomplished, justice served.

But all this is vicarious. It takes place entirely in our imagination. More important, WE KNOW THAT IT DOES. Before the credits have finished running up the screen, we have returned to everyday life, ready to wash the car, take out the garbage, or turn to our studies. The fictional encounter with violence is not only out of sight but also out of mind.

⏩ Exercise 36 (cont.)

The proof that TV violence does not stay in the mind is found in a simple fact. Though virtually everyone sees violence on TV and in films, only a small percentage of people, surely less than 1 percent, ever commit a violent crime. Since the vast majority are unaffected by what they view on TV, the cause of violence must lie in the minds of the tiny minority. Those people would no doubt be violent even if they never watched a TV program. Something else would trigger their aberrant behavior, such as *Grimm's Fairy Tales* or a newspaper account of a crime.

Has anyone ever produced a shred of evidence linking TV viewing and violent behavior? I've never seen it, nor has anyone else because there is none. It exists only in the minds of the would-be censors. Those people have a right to watch whatever they want to watch on TV and to set restrictions on what their kids watch. If they wish, they can toss their TV set out on the village dump and spend their evenings reading or playing Monopoly. What they don't have a right to do is to dictate what is available for the rest of us to see.

⏩ Exercise 37

Many campuses have adopted speech codes to ensure an atmosphere of respect and civility. However, these codes have given rise to controversy. Some see them as helpful and even necessary. Others regard them as an exercise in foolishness or, worse, a violation of their constitutional rights. Analyze this issue using the five-step approach detailed in this chapter and present your findings on a separate sheet of paper. Following are two opposing viewpoints on this issue to get you started:

Campus Speech Codes Are Reasonable
By Priscilla Prentice

A generation ago, rage was an uncommon word. Today it is not only common— it comes in a number of varieties. We have road rage, in which drivers become furious at fellow motorists for real or imagined violations of the rules of the road. We have air rage, in which passengers on airplanes take out their frustrations on other passengers or flight attendants and have to be restrained. And we have sports-event rage, characterized by fans leaping onto the playing field and pummeling someone, usually a player or official or, in the case of little league competitions, the coach who didn't give little Johnny or Sally sufficient playing time.

⬢ Exercise 37 (cont.)

We also have campus rage, which may be defined as the practice of intimidating and harassing students or faculty one doesn't like. Typically, the victim of this kind of rage is a member of a minority group—for example, homosexuals, African Americans, Latinos, or Muslims. Campus rage tends to be expressed in epithets and insults rather than in physical assaults, so the wounds it causes are invisible. But they are no less real or less lasting for that fact.

Campus speech codes are a sensitive and sensible response to campus rage. They make understandable to everyone at what point commentary on an idea or issue ends and attacks on individuals begin, marking the latter as impermissible. When such codes are well written, they also inform everyone exactly what the penalties will be for violations. The only people who *should* be against campus speech codes are irresponsible individuals who don't care about other people's feelings. I mean people who have something to fear from them—the kind of people who scrawl hate messages on buildings; use ugly, demeaning terms to describe other human beings; and spread stereotypes and vicious rumors.

To be fair, some honest people are against speech codes. But their arguments are flawed. The most significant of those arguments is that campus speech codes violate the right to free speech. There is an element of truth—albeit a small one—in that argument. Any regulation, rule, or law sets a limit on behavior. For example, a traffic light makes us stop when we want to continue going forward. The designation "one-way street" restricts our freedom to go the other way. Airport security requirements require us to submit to questions we would rather not answer and searches we would rather not submit to. But responsible people don't object to these restrictions because they understand that the restrictions serve a purpose that is higher and more important than any individual's convenience.

Campus speech codes should be viewed in the same light. They do limit our right to free speech in a minor way. Yet they do so in order to honor another, equally important right: the potential victim's right to the pursuit of happiness. The idea behind campus speech codes is simply this—just as no one is allowed to assault others physically, no one should be permitted to assault others verbally. Nothing could be more reasonable than that.

Campus Speech Codes Are Intolerable
By Zachariah Brescia

Campus speech codes come wrapped in idealistic language. They supposedly aim to create an environment where fairness reigns, no one's feelings are ever hurt, and everyone feels comfortable. What could possibly be wrong with that? Plenty.

To begin with, campus speech codes are not about fairness at all but privilege. And they are not about soothing feelings but suppressing ideas that don't pass the test of Political Correctness. Anyone who takes the unpopular side of an issue is shouted down or assigned an ugly label. Those who speak against affirmative action are branded racists. Those who oppose gay marriage are called homophobes. Those who speak out against abortion are branded "anti-choice." (So much for being concerned about people's feelings.)

On most campuses, it is permissible to say "all men are rapists," "George W. Bush is a war criminal," and "the United States deserved what happened on September 11, 2001" but not to challenge those ideas. Similarly, denouncing religion is acceptable, whereas praising or—GASP!—*professing* a religious belief is considered an outrage.

The punishment doesn't end with name calling and denunciation either. The Politically Correct crowd have also borrowed a tactic from their ideological mentors, the communists. The tactic is called "re-education," but its real meaning is brainwashing. For example, on many campuses people who challenge the liberal dogma of Diversity are required to undergo "diversity training," which consists of sitting silently and being "persuaded" of one's error.

An even more creative trick is to establish "free speech zones" on campus—that is, special places where people can go whenever they want and say whatever they want. At first thought, this sounds perfectly reasonable. Only when you ponder the idea for a while and ask pertinent questions do you realize what's happening. *Question: Where will these "free speech zones" be?* In front of the administration building? At the fountain in the center of campus? Behind the sewage treatment plant? *Question: Will the number and size of these zones ever change?* For example, if the people who use the zones vigorously question Politically Correct ideas, will the zones get fewer and fewer and smaller and smaller?

Questions such as these expose the nature of the game being played. Speech code advocates are pretending to *give* something to the campus community (free speech zones) when they are really taking something away (free speech). Listen carefully and you'll be able to hear the Founding Fathers turning over in their graves. (Incidentally, "Founding Fathers" is politically incorrect because it omits mothers.) When those wise men wrote the U.S. Constitution they were espousing the free expression of ideas, even ones that some people find offensive. They believed that the way to conquer bad ideas is not by suppression but by countering them with good ideas. If they were with us today, they would condemn campus speech codes. And so should we.

⬛▶ Exercise 38

Analyze ONE of the following issues using the five-step approach detailed in this chapter. In conducting your research, be especially careful to find and examine viewpoints that differ from the one presented. Using a separate sheet of paper, write a composition presenting your findings.

The Government's Role in Gambling

By Natalia Slavinsky

The man waits nervously in the long line of people. He's already late for work, and he knows the boss will be angry with him. But he's determined not to leave; he has a strong feeling that this will be the luckiest day of his life. What could possibly be important enough to risk offending one's employer? Buying a ticket on the lottery.

Today's lottery operations and their companion enterprises, off-track betting parlors, are big business. Government officials see them as ideal ways to raise billions of dollars in revenue without raising taxes. The reasoning is that since many people enjoy gambling and no one is hurt by it, there's nothing wrong with the government's taking a piece of the action and using the proceeds to benefit the public.

That reasoning is mistaken. Gambling is a vice. People are hurt by it. It's wrong for the government to be involved in it—every bit as wrong as it would be for the government to run a chain of brothels or a tobacco company or a liquor distillery.

Addiction to gambling is no less a disease than alcoholism. People afflicted by it do not act freely when they place a bet; they are compelled to do so. And they aren't the only ones hurt when they throw away their money: their spouses and children also suffer. Money that could buy food and clothing, pay the rent, or buy dental care is invested in the childish expectation of beating the odds.

The advertisements for the lottery and off-track betting are cleverly crafted to create the impression that the bettor has a good chance of winning. For example, one commercial begins with the words to an old song, "Fairy tales can come true, it can happen to you . . ." and goes on to dramatize the experience of winning. Slogans like "You can't win it if you're not in it" tease bettors to buy a ticket. And the one in ten or twenty million people who happens to win a big jackpot has his or her picture in the paper and is an instant celebrity, whereas the losers are never mentioned.

If the government used such tactics to tempt alcoholics or smokers, people would be outraged. Rightly so. The government's proper role is to safeguard the people's rights, not to profit from their weakness and gullibility. The fact that the proceeds from gambling are put to good use in no way diminishes the offense of government involvement in it.

A Disservice to Everyone
By Bruce Malone

Talk-show TV often displays a mindlessness that's as amazing as it is appalling. One show, for example, featured teenagers who had decided to drop out of high school. The program began with the teens presenting their reasons for quitting, then proceeded to have their parents, a guest expert, and the host try to persuade them to stay in school. Finally, the teens were given a chance to answer the arguments of their elders.

If the show's host and producers thought they were helping solve the problem of high school dropouts, they were mistaken. Appearing on television is an honor few people receive, even if they have made significant contributions to society. Yet those teens received just that honor for threatening to drop out of school. Their foolishness was dignified and they were made to feel like celebrities. Worse, by being allowed to have the last word on the issue, they were given an advantage over the adults.

The chances that those teens changed their minds after the program are slim to none. They very likely had the show videotaped and ran the tape over and over, showing their friends how they held their own in the debate. They may even fantasize that a career in television awaits them. It's not hard to imagine them becoming the heroes of the neighborhood.

Such programs make the jobs of parents and teachers more difficult. Popular culture has already convinced many young people that they know more than their elders, that their opinions have special value, and that learning is a waste of time. Television shows that reinforce such nonsense are surely not a public service. If anything, they are a public disservice.

☑ quiz

Write your answers on a separate sheet of paper.

1. Would it be accurate to define an argument as a dispute characterized by angry exchanges? Explain.

2. What is the most important resource available in any library?

3. What contribution did Melvil Dewey make to critical thinking?

4. A search engine is a large machine librarians use to find books that have been improperly shelved. True or false? Explain.

5. Questions calling for a simple yes or no answer are most effective in an interview. True or false? Explain.

6. List the three steps you can take to avoid plagiarism.

7. List three kinds of evidence and the questions appropriate for testing each.

8. Where is the central opinion in an article usually found?

9. Explain how "and' relationships, "but" relationships, and "therefore" relationships differ.

10. List the five steps in the approach for evaluating complex issues.

11. When you evaluate an argument, the greatest obstacle to critical thinking is the complexity of the issue. True or false? Explain.

Answers to this quiz may be found at http://college.hmco.com.

CHAPTER **5**

Recognizing Errors in Thinking

IN THIS CHAPTER:

Three kinds of errors — *Be alert for errors of perception, judgment, and reaction.*

Errors of perception — *Errors often begin in faulty ways of seeing the world—"mine is better" thinking, selective perception, gullibility and skepticism, bias, pretending to know, and either/or thinking.*

Errors of judgment — *Double standard, irrelevant criterion, overgeneralizing or stereotyping, hasty conclusion, unwarranted assumption, failure to make a distinction, and oversimplification are the main kinds of judgment errors.*

Errors of reaction — *When we explain away ideas, shift the burden of proof, attack the person, or set up a "straw man," we risk fooling ourselves.*

Errors can multiply — *Any error in thinking invites additional errors.*

Three kinds of errors

> *Most often people seek in life occasions for persisting in their opinions rather than for educating themselves. Each of us looks for justification in the event. The rest, which runs counter to that opinion, is overlooked. . . . It seems as if the mind enjoys nothing more than sinking deeper into error.*
> —ANDRÉ GIDE

Perhaps Gide overstated the problem in suggesting that we *enjoy* error. But he was wise in noting our difficulty in dealing with issues objectively and logically. To overcome that difficulty, we need to understand the kinds of errors that can entrap us and the steps we can take to avoid them.

Three broad types of errors are common: errors of perception, errors of judgment, and errors of reaction:

Errors of perception

Errors of perception are not blunders made while examining issues. They are faulty ways of seeing reality, preventing us from being open-minded even before we begin to apply our critical thinking. The following are especially serious:

"Mine is better" thinking

As small children we may have said "My mommy is prettier than any other mommy" or "My daddy is bigger and stronger." Perhaps we had similar thoughts about our houses, toys, and finger paintings.

Now that we've gotten older, we probably don't express "mine is better" thinking. Yet we may still indulge in it. Such thinking often occurs

in matters that are important to us, such as our race, religion, ethnic group, social class, political party, or philosophy of life.

This habit is not always obvious. In fact, "mine is better" thinking can be very subtle. We may be very uninterested in a person until we find out she is Irish, like us. Suddenly we feel a sense of kinship. We may think a person is rather dense until he says something that matches our view. Then we decide he's really quite bright after all.

"Mine is better" thinking is natural and often harmless. Even so, this kind of thinking creates distance between people through a win-lose mentality, which can easily prevent you from learning from others. To prevent this from happening, remember that opening your mind to ideas from other people can broaden your perspective and lead to fresh insights. Give every idea a fair hearing—even an idea that challenges your own.

Selective perception

In one sense, we see selectively most of the time. Let's say you and two friends, a horticulture major and an art major, walk through a shopping mall. You want to buy a pair of shoes; the others are just taking a break from studying. The same reality exists for each of you: stores, potted plants, people passing by. Still, each of you focuses on different things. While you are looking for shoe stores, one friend notices plants. The other studies faces for interesting features.

Later, one of you says, "Hey, did you see the big new store in the mall?" The others say no. Though the store was before all of your eyes, two of you screened it out.

That kind of selective perception is often harmless. Another kind of selective perception takes place when we focus on things that support our current ideas and reject anything that challenges them. Suppose someone thinks that a particular ethnic group is stupid, violent, cheap, or lazy. Then "stupid" behaviors will capture that person's attention. And if his bias is strong enough, he will completely miss intelligent behaviors from members of that group. He'll see only evidence that supports his prejudice.

You can break the habit of selective perception by looking and listening for details you haven't seen before. Also press yourself to balance your perception. If you find yourself focusing on negative details, look for positive ones, and vice versa.

Gullibility and skepticism

Philosopher Alfred Korzybski observed, "there are two ways to slide easily through life: to believe everything or to doubt everything—both ways save us from thinking." To believe everything we are told is to be gullible. To doubt everything is to be skeptical.

An alternative to gullibility and skepticism is questioning. This means greeting all ideas with curiosity and wonder, judging none of them in advance, and being equally prepared to find wisdom, foolishness, or some combination of the two.

▶ Good Thinking!

The Story of Paul Vitz

Paul C. Vitz is a professor of psychology and the author of many articles and several books, including *Faith of the Fatherless: The Psychology of Atheism*. The story behind this book illustrates how a simple question can lead to new insights.

For much of his life, Vitz had been an atheist, but at age 38 he embraced religion and became interested in the historic tension between psychology and religion. He learned that, "even in intellectual and academic circles, atheism did not become respectable until about 1870 . . . and it continued to be restricted to small numbers of intellectuals into the twentieth century." From his training as a psychologist he also knew that "many atheists are famous for arguing that [religious] believers suffer from illusions, from unconscious and infantile needs, and from other psychological deficits." Freud, for example, argued that belief in God is nothing more than a projection of the believer's desire for security.

As he reflected on these facts, he began to wonder whether this "projection theory" might apply to atheists as well as to believers, or perhaps even apply *better* to atheists than to believers. Eager to find out, he decided to study the lives of famous atheists and famous religious believers and see if any interesting patterns emerged. The atheists he chose included Freud, Nietzsche, Hume, and Sartre; the theists included Pascal, Berkeley, de Tocqueville, Kierkegaard, and Buber.

This study revealed that every famous atheist had a weak, dead, or abusive father, and almost every theist had a positive relationship with his father. After analyzing the data, Vitz concluded that the projection theory of religious belief is not only unscientific but also a form of the logical fallacy known as *ad hominem*— in other words, it focuses on the believer personally rather than on the evidence for and/or against religious belief.

Vitz writes as follows: "Since *both* believers and nonbelievers in God have psychological reasons for their positions, one important conclusion is that in any debate as to the truth of the existence of God, psychology should be irrelevant. A genuine search for evidence supporting, or opposing, the existence of God should be based on the evidence and arguments found in philosophy, theology, science, history, and other relevant disciplines. It should also include an understanding of religious experience."

Paul Vitz's research could pave the way for a more scholarly approach to the study of religion.

For more information on Paul Vitz, see Paul Vitz, *Faith of the Fatherless: The Psychology of Atheism* (Dallas, TX: Spence Publishing Co., 1999).

Bias

Bias toward the majority or the minority. Bias tends to follow our affections. If we feel more comfortable with the majority on our side, we may choose the majority view. If we identify with the underdog and love the challenge of confronting superior numbers, we may embrace the minority view.

Each of these choices can occur with little or no awareness of our underlying bias. And in each case we put feelings of comfort and personal preference above the evidence. Critical thinking means deciding issues on their merits rather than on the number or the celebrity status of the people on the opposing sides.

Bias for or against change. According to an old joke, conservatives have never met a new idea they liked, and liberals have never met a new idea they didn't like. Each observation contains an element of truth.

Some people find even small changes, like returning home from school and finding the furniture rearranged, very upsetting. Major changes, like moving across the country, can be even more disturbing.

New ideas can have a similar effect on such people. Old beliefs provide a sense of comfort and security. When those beliefs are challenged, people may feel that reality has been pulled out from under them. That's probably why ancient rulers killed the bearers of bad news. It's also one reason why persuading others can be difficult.

Bias against change may be older and more common than bias for change. Yet the latter seems to be increasing today, perhaps because technology is advancing so rapidly. Some people think that old ideas, old beliefs, and old values are of little use today. For them, new is always better.

Neither perspective is consistent with critical thinking. Some new ideas are clearly better than the old ones they replace. Progress has in fact occurred in every area of life, including science, technology, education, and government. Yet this reality has another, less beneficial side. New ideas can contain serious flaws that go unnoticed at first. Time and experience can prove that the supposed great leap forward was actually several steps backward.

To avoid bias for or against change, know your own mental habits. Also resist the temptation to accept first impressions.

Pretending to know

Some people believe that confessing ignorance makes them look in-effective, so they pretend to know things. After a while, pretending becomes a habit that hinders critical thinking. Suppose someone says on several occasions, "I've read quite a few books on psychology." Also sup-pose the truth is different and he's never read a book on the subject. The idea will become so familiar that he might take it for the truth. What's more, he'll begin to confuse his guesses about psychology with real knowledge. Practice staying aware of your statements and remaining alert for pretense. Whenever you find it, acknowledge the truth and resolve not to lie to yourself or others again.

Either/or thinking

This error of perception means taking only extreme positions on an issue when other positions are possible. For example, one person thinks that accepting evolution means rejecting the idea of creation. Another person thinks that being Republican means taking a conservative stance on every issue.

Yet it's possible to believe in evolution and creation. You could believe that God created the universe and planned for it to evolve over millions of years. (You could also be a Republican without always taking a con-servative stand.)

Either/or thinking hampers critical thinking. This error prompts us to take extreme, unreasonable views. To avoid either/or thinking, look for times when there seem to be only two possible views. Ask yourself, "Are these the only possibilities? Could another view be more reasonable—per-haps one that includes elements of both?"

An example is the debate over crime prevention. Some elected offi-cials argue for banning assault weapons and registering handguns. The National Rifle Association argues for getting criminals off the street. You might ask, "Why not take both actions and add others, such as building more prisons, as well?"

⬛▶ Exercise 39

Consider each of the seven errors of perception. Think of a time when you've committed each one and describe the situation. Explain how you reacted and what consequences followed. Then decide how you might have avoided the error and how the consequences could have been different.

"Mine is better" thinking

_____

_____

_____

⏩ Exercise 39 (cont.)

Selective perception

_____

_____

_____

Gullibility and skepticism

_____

_____

_____

Bias

_____

_____

_____

Pretending to know

_____

_____

_____

Either/or thinking

_____

_____

_____

Errors of judgment

Errors of judgment occur in the process of sorting out and assessing evidence. They prevent us from reaching the most reasonable conclusion. The following errors of judgment are among the most common:

Double standard

This error consists of using one standard of judgment for our ideas and an entirely different, more demanding standard for ideas that conflict with ours.

People who employ a double standard ignore inconsistencies, contradictions, and outrageous overstatements in arguments they agree with. Yet they nitpick their opponents' arguments. They even use different vocabularies. Allies are described as "imaginative," "forceful," and "brutally honest." Opponents with the same qualities are labeled "utopian," "belligerent," or "mean-spirited."

Critical thinking demands a single standard of judgment for both those who agree and those who disagree with us.

Irrelevant criterion

This error consists of criticizing an idea because it fails to do what it wasn't intended to do. Say that a chief executive proposes a new reward program for employees' cost-saving ideas in his company. Supervisors argue against the program because it doesn't increase the percentage of women and minorities in the company. In this case, the supervisors are invoking an irrelevant criterion.

The point is not that fairness to women and minorities is unimportant. Rather, fairness is a different issue and should not be made the measure of the reward program.

You can avoid the mistake of using irrelevant criteria. When you evaluate an idea, set aside all separate issues and agendas, no matter how important they are or how committed you feel about them.

Overgeneralizing or stereotyping

Generalizations are judgments about a class of people or things. Political pollsters are generalizing when they say, "Most voters don't care much about either presidential candidate." Though such a statement covers tens of millions of people, it's a fair one if based on a representative sample of those people.

Generalizations don't have to be based on a scientific sampling in order to be fair. They need only be based on a reasonable number of contacts with a reasonable number of people in the group. For example, your instructor might say, "My present students are more willing to participate in class than my students were last year." Or you could say, "The people in my neighborhood are friendly."

Overgeneralizations are unfair generalizations. They exceed what's appropriate to conclude from our experiences. Suppose a professor teaches only advanced French literature and sees only a small, unique group of students. If she says something about "the students at this college" based solely on her experience, she is thinking uncritically. Or consider a first semester student who has contact with only five instructors. This person would be overgeneralizing if he judged "the faculty at this school."

Stereotypes are overgeneralizations that harden into convictions shared by many people. There are stereotypes of people: fundamentalists, politicians, feminists, psychiatrists, rock musicians. And there are stereotypes of places and things: New York City and San Francisco, marriage and farming.

Overgeneralizations and stereotypes hinder critical thinking by blinding us to important differences among individual people, places, and things.

▶ Good Thinking!

The Story of Carol Tavris

As psychologist Carol Tavris considered all the books and tapes claiming there are profound differences between the sexes, she wondered: How accurate are such descriptions? What research are they based on? Are they developing genuine understanding? Is it possible that they are perpetuating or, worse, *inventing* myths?

Her wondering led her to investigate and, eventually, to present her findings in a book entitled *The Mismeasure of Woman*. One finding was that the variation in mathematical ability between individual women (or individual men) is greater than the variation between women in general and men in general. The same is true of verbal ability. This finding explodes the common notion that men are more talented in math and women are more talented in language.

Another of Tavris's findings was that traits such as sympathy, empathy, and nurturing are related to the task of caregiving rather than to gender. Caregivers, both male and female, tend to have these traits more than non-caregivers do. Thus, an unmarried man who cares for an elderly or ailing parent is likely to be more caring than an unmarried woman who has no such responsibilities.

A third finding challenged the popular idea that the basis of women's moral reasoning is compassion but the basis of men's is justice. Research confirms that compassion and justice are used in the moral reasoning of both sexes, more or less equally.

The results of her investigation led Tavris to conclude that popular thinking about female and male traits is, in some important ways, erroneous. She writes: "Under some conditions the qualities we label feminine are good for both sexes, and under some conditions the qualities we label masculine are good for both sexes." In family situations, she argues, *both* sexes should show "compassion, nurturance, and warmth"; and in the workplace, *both* should show "assertiveness, competence, and self-confidence."

In Tavris's view, "the goal for both sexes should be to add qualities and skills, not lose old ones."

For more information on Carol Tavris, see Carol Tavris, *The Mismeasure of Woman* (New York: Simon & Schuster, 1992).

Hasty conclusion

Hasty conclusions are those drawn without enough evidence. Consider this case: A student often leaves the door to his room open and many people have access to the room. One day he discovers an expensive pen is missing from his desk. He concludes that his roommate took it. This is a hasty conclusion. It's possible that his roommate stole the pen. It's also possible that someone else stole it. Or perhaps he lost or misplaced the pen.

In many cases, two or more conclusions are possible. Critical thinking means having a good reason for choosing one over the others. If no such reason exists, suspend judgment and seek more evidence.

Unwarranted assumption

Assumptions are ideas we take for granted. They differ from conclusions in an important way: Assumptions are *implied* rather than expressed. In many cases we make them unconsciously. Consider this exchange:

> *Sally:* You say that discrimination against women is a thing of the past. That's just not true.
>
> *Ralph:* It certainly is true. I read it in a magazine.

Ralph may not be aware of it, but he is assuming that whatever appears in a magazine is necessarily true. This assumption takes too much for granted, so it is unwarranted.

There's nothing necessarily wrong with assumptions. Making them allows us to conduct our daily activities efficiently. When you got up this morning, you assumed there would be enough hot water to take a shower. If you drove to school, you probably assumed that your car would start and your instructors would hold classes. Unless there was a good reason not to make these assumptions—for example, if you knew your water heater was broken—they would be valid.

The assumptions that hinder critical thinking are unwarranted assumptions. They prevent us from asking useful questions and exploring possibilities. For example, if a student assumes that it is the teacher's job to make class interesting, she is unlikely to ask herself, "What responsibility do my fellow students and I have to make class interesting?" Here are some common unwarranted assumptions:

Unwarranted Assumption	*Why Unwarranted*
People's senses are always trustworthy.	Sometimes people's beliefs are in error.
Having reasons proves that one has reasoned carefully.	Some reasons are not thought out at all but simply borrowed from others.
Conviction constitutes proof.	It is possible to be passionately committed to a mistaken idea.
Familiar ideas are more valid than unfamiliar ideas.	If we hear a false statement often enough, it becomes familiar and we naturally regard it as true.
If one event occurs soon after another, it must have been caused by the other.	Sometimes the closeness in time is merely coincidental.
The way things are is the way they are supposed to be.	Because we humans are an imperfect species, what we invent or establish is almost always open to improvement.
Whatever hasn't been done is impossible to do.	According to Edward Karsner and James Newman, "the first steam vessel to cross the Atlantic carried, as part of its cargo, a book which 'proved' that it was impossible for a steam vessel to cross anything, much less the Atlantic" (Larrabee, 91). The author of that book obviously assumed that what hadn't yet been done couldn't be done.
If an idea is in one's mind, it must have originated there.	All day long, every day of our lives, we read and hear other people's ideas. Those we hear only once may be quickly forgotten, but those we hear many times are reinforced, especially when we repeat them in our own words. In time we may mistakenly regard them as uniquely ours.

Widely accepted ideas must be true.

Nations and cultures can be as easily mistaken as individuals. History is filled with examples, such as the popular notion that high self-esteem is correlated with success and low self-esteem with failure. Harold Stevenson and James Stigler tested this idea in a study of elementary students from Japan, Taiwan, China, and the United States. All the Asian students outperformed the Americans academically yet scored lower in self-esteem (Stevenson). Moreover, in 1990 a group of scholars, many of them favorably disposed to the self-esteem theory, reviewed the research on self-esteem and found, in the words of sociologist Neil Smelser, "the associations between self-esteem and its expected consequences are mixed, insignificant, or absent" (Kohn, 274).

Because assumptions are unstated and often unconscious, they are difficult to detect. When you look for assumptions in your own thinking and writing, go beyond what you consciously thought or wrote. Ask yourself, "What am I not expressing but merely taking for granted?"

Failure to make a distinction

Distinctions are subtle differences among things. Care in making distinctions can help you overcome confusion and deal with complex issues effectively. Following are some important distinctions to recognize:

The Distinction	*Why Necessary*
The distinction between the person and the idea.	Critical thinkers judge an idea on its own merits—not on the celebrity status or expertise of the person expressing it. Though experts usually have more informed views than novices, experts can be wrong and novices can have genuine insights.

The distinction between assertion and evidence.	Some people pile assertion upon assertion without evidence. If these people are articulate, the casual thinker may be persuaded. Critical thinkers judge ideas on how well supported—and supportable—they are. This is more important than how well the idea is expressed.
The distinction between familiarity and validity.	We're naturally attracted to the familiar. It's easy to believe that reasoning is valid merely because we've heard it many times. Critical thinkers, however, are not swayed by familiarity.
The distinction between often *and* always, seldom *and* never.	Uncritical thinkers tend to ignore this distinction. They might say something "always" occurs when the evidence supports only "often," or they might say it "never" occurs when the evidence supports only "seldom." Critical thinkers are careful to make the distinction.

Oversimplification

There's nothing wrong with simplifying. In elementary school especially, teachers simplify their subjects. Professionals such as engineers and chemists simplify to communicate with people untrained in their fields.

Oversimplification differs from simplification. Oversimplification omits essential information or ignores complexity. Consider this idea: "High school teachers have it made. They're through at three o'clock every day and work only nine months of the year." Though there is some truth to this statement, it's inaccurate. Teachers often prepare four or five classes a day, grade homework, keep records, chaperone activities, and advise organizations. These activities often occur outside the normal eight-hour day. In addition, teachers are often required to take summer courses.

Oversimplification distorts reality and confuses discussion.

▶ Exercise 40

Consider each of the seven errors of judgment. Think of a time when you've committed each, and describe the situation. Explain how you reacted and what events followed. Then decide how you could have avoided each error and how the consequences might have been different.

Double standard

_____

_____

_____

Irrelevant criterion

_____

_____

_____

Overgeneralizing or stereotyping

_____

_____

_____

Hasty conclusion

_____

_____

_____

Unwarranted assumption

_____

_____

_____

Failure to make a distinction

_____

_____

_____

⏩ Exercise 40 (cont.)

Oversimplification

_____

_____

_____

⏩ Exercise 41

Read each of the following passages carefully, looking for errors of judgment. When you find one, explain the error in the space provided.

A.

Sue: My English instructor makes us rewrite any composition that contains more than three errors in grammar or usage. And she's always demanding that we do better in our writing. I think she dislikes us.

Ellen: I know what you mean. The professors at this college seem to think it's Harvard.

_____

_____

_____

B.

Morris: Did you notice all the people using food stamps in the grocery store this morning?

Olaf: Yeah. It seems everybody has them these days. It's the fashionable thing to plead poverty.

Morris: That one woman was dressed well, too. I'll bet her lazy husband was waiting for her outside in a big fancy car.

Olaf: It makes me sick, people like that leeching on society. Darwin had the right idea: survival of the fittest. If people can't survive on their own, let them suffer.

_____

_____

_____

 Exercise 41 (cont.)

C.

Times change, and values in one age are different from values in another. Parents fail to realize this. That's why they keep harping about avoiding alcohol and drugs and postponing sexual involvement. They think that what was right for them is right for us.

_____

_____

_____

D.

Boris: Can you believe the price of textbooks? The average amount I spent for a book this semester was $45, and a good half of my books are paperbacks.

Elaine: Everybody's complaining about it. When the cost of books keeps going up and up, there's only one explanation: The authors and publishers are getting greedy.

Boris: Yeah, and you know one of my instructors has the nerve to make us buy a book he wrote. And get this: He teaches Ethics!

Elaine: Wow.

_____

_____

_____

E.

Zeb: Did you read the latest about Senator Fosdick? The candidate running against him claimed he knowingly received illegal campaign contributions.

Clarissa: How ironic. Senator Fosdick has been talking about campaign reform for years. Now it turns out he's as big a crook as the rest of them. What a hypocrite.

_____

_____

_____

▶ Exercise 41 (cont.)

F.

 Cynthia: A study has shown that as the speed limit has been raised, there's been an increase in traffic fatalities.

 Mark: Speed limits don't cause traffic fatalities. Careless drivers do.

_____

_____

_____

G.

 Abdul: Any athlete who physically attacks his coach shouldn't just receive a fine. He should be arrested and charged with assault.

 Simon: I disagree. No player attacks a coach without good reason. Besides, coaches are too negative, telling players what to do and yelling at them when they make mistakes. That behavior invites physical attack.

_____

_____

_____

H.

 Saul: Hey, Paul, why so glum?

 Paul: "I can't believe it. I got a 'D' on that paper after I spent four hours on it. The instructor must really have it in for me."

_____

_____

_____

I.

 Juwan: Ever since I arrived on campus last month, I've been appalled by the manners of the students here. They're unbelievably boorish.

 Samantha: Right. And the townspeople are so unfriendly. I don't know why I ever picked this college.

 Juwan: Oh, I'm not sorry I came. The professors are helpful and encouraging. They go out of their way to explain things.

_____

_____

_____

Errors of reaction

Errors of reaction occur when we express a viewpoint and someone reacts negatively. They are defensive reactions that preserve our self image and provide an excuse to maintain our view. The following errors of reaction are the most common.

Explaining away

Ron has been a marijuana smoker for several years. He maintains that marijuana is harmless. Last night he and a group of friends were talking, and one of them mentioned that his health instructor had distributed an article from the *Journal of the American Medical Association.*

That article reported the results of a clinical study of marijuana use. It concluded that "contrary to what is frequently reported, we have found the effect of marijuana to be not merely that of a mild intoxicant which causes a slight exaggeration of usual adolescent behavior, but a specific and separate clinical syndrome." The main effects the study noted were "disturbed awareness of the self, apathy, confusion and poor reality testing."

Ron's reply was heated. "Those articles are written by a bunch of guys who never smoked a joint. They're guessing, fantasizing, or worse, making up scare stories for parents to feed their kiddies. I've smoked pot for years, and I can tell you it's had no effect on me."

Ron found the prospect of being wrong about marijuana and the possibility of injuring himself too unpleasant to consider. This is understandable. Still, critical thinking would suggest that he at least read the article and examine the evidence. Instead, he resorted to a tactic long used in uncritical thinking: explain it away.

When people explain away challenges to their ideas, they don't change reality. They just postpone dealing with it. The longer they postpone, the more painful the experience. If you wish to avoid such results, face unpleasant ideas directly and honestly.

Shifting the burden of proof

Accepting the burden of proof means supporting our assertions. The more the assertions challenge accepted wisdom, the greater the burden. What's more, this burden falls on the person who makes the assertion. Here's how this concept applies in an actual case. Two students are discussing greatness in boxing:

> *Zeke:* Mike Tyson was the greatest heavyweight boxer of all time.
> *Brad:* Wait a minute. There have been a lot of great heavyweights over the years. I doubt Tyson was better than all of them.
> *Zeke:* I stand by my position. Prove me wrong if you can.

There would be nothing wrong with Zeke's asking Brad why he doubts Tyson's greatness. But when Zeke says "Prove me wrong," he's shifting the burden of proof. Since Zeke made the original statement, he should be prepared to defend it.

When you make an assertion, you might be called on to defend it. And if you find that you can't defend the assertion, avoid shifting your burden of proof. Instead, withdraw the assertion.

Attacking the person

In uncritical thinking there's a common way of reacting to challenges: attack the challenger. Here's a common scenario.

Mclissa argues that it makes no sense for students to vote while they're away at college. The process of obtaining an absentee ballot is time consuming, she says. And with so many people voting, a student's vote isn't that important.

Agnes challenges Melissa's view. "I voted by absentee ballot last year," she says, "and the process was simple." Agnes adds that some elections are close enough to be decided by a few thousand votes. What's more, hundreds of thousands of college students are eligible to vote.

Now Melissa is embarrassed. The weakness of her view has been exposed in front of other students. She launches an attack on Agnes. "You have no business lecturing me about right and wrong. Just last week you cut Friday's classes so you could go home early, and then you lied to your instructors about being sick. Stop being a hypocrite, Agnes."

Even if this attack on Agnes is true, it has nothing to do with the issue of college students voting. It's merely a way for Melissa to save face.

How would Melissa respond if she practiced critical thinking? She would focus on Agnes's idea rather than on Agnes as a person. And since the idea seems reasonable, Melissa would probe it further before dismissing it. She could say, "Perhaps I'm mistaken. What steps are needed to vote by absentee ballot?" Then if Agnes's answer showed that the process was simple, Melissa could respond, "I guess you're right."

By acting this way, Melissa would not lose face. In fact, the other students might be impressed at her flexibility and willingness to admit a mistake

Straw man

This error involves make-believe. Specifically, the error means pretending someone has said something that he or she has not said, and then denouncing him or her for saying it.

Imagine this situation: Someone has proposed that your school's attendance policy be revised to permit unlimited absences from class without penalty. You argue against the proposal, claiming that students who attend class sporadically slow the pace of learning for others and degrade the quality of class discussion.

Then someone responds to your argument as follows: "I take exception to your view. You say that adults should be treated as children, that students must leave their constitutional rights at the college gate, and that individuals whose work obligations sometimes force them to miss class are inferior creatures deserving of punishment."

Those stirring words, which bear no relation to reality, constitute the error of straw man. They attribute to you something you did not say. To avoid the error of straw man, listen to or read others' arguments carefully. Focus your criticism on what was actually said or clearly implied.

In all these errors of reaction, ego gets in the way of critical thinking. It's in your long-term interest to acknowledge error and learn from it. Doing so promotes knowledge and wisdom.

▨ Exercise 42

Consider each of the four errors of reaction. Think of a time when you committed each and describe the situation. Explain how you reacted and what consequences resulted. Then decide how you might have avoided the error and how the consequences might have been different. (If you can't think of an error of your own, identify one you encountered through reading or observation.)

Explaining away

_____

_____

_____

Shifting the burden of proof

_____

_____

_____

Attacking the person

_____

_____

_____

Straw man

_____

_____

_____

▶ Exercise 43

Reflect on the following observation, then record your thoughts in the space provided.

OBSERVATION

Psychologist Abraham Maslow explained the hierarchy of human needs by using the figure of a pyramid (see illustration). The lower needs, he believed, must be met before the higher needs are pursued. At the bottom of his pyramid are physiological needs (food, clothing, shelter). Then comes the need for belongingness and love. Above that comes self-esteem, then aesthetic and intellectual needs. At the top, representing the highest need, is self-actualization.

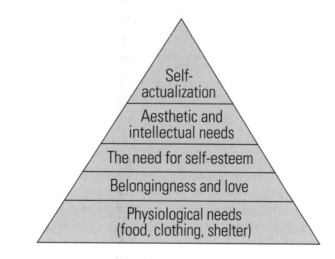

Austrian psychiatrist Viktor Frankl challenged this order. He argued that self-transcendence—forgetting about self and seeking challenging tasks to add meaning to one's existence—is the highest human need. He also believed that self-actualization cannot be pursued but comes only by achieving self-transcendence. Several decades have passed since these two views were first presented, and in the United States Maslow's has been more influential.

REFLECTION

_____

_____

_____

_____

_____

Exercise 44

Reflect on the following observation, then record your thoughts in the space provided.

OBSERVATION

Many people reason that because everyone has a right to his or her opinion, everyone's opinion should be treated with respect and never challenged or disputed.

REFLECTION

_____

_____

_____

_____

_____

Errors can multiply

Errors would be costly enough if they occurred singly and separately. Yet in many cases one error invites another and that leads to several more. It's natural for us to want knowledge and wisdom. (Have you ever met anyone who *wanted* to be ignorant and foolish?) And its easy to go from wanting it to pretending we have it and then to seeing the world in a way that reinforces our pretense.

Such a chain of perception errors paves the way for errors of judgment. For example, are we assuming too much, ignoring important distinctions, and jumping to conclusions that flatter our viewpoint. And once we embrace errors of judgment, express them to others, and hear them criticized, we are tempted to commit errors of reaction to save face.

Remembering the ways in which errors tend to multiply can keep you motivated to think critically.

⧫ Exercise 45

Should "illegal aliens" be accorded the same rights as U.S. citizens? The debate over this issue has become intense since the "9/11" attack on the World Trade Center. Analyze this issue using the five-step approach detailed in Chapter Four. Following are two opposing viewpoints on this issue to get you started.

Laws Are Meant to Be Observed
By Kareem Ali

An alien in a country is a person who lives there but whose home is in another country. An illegal alien is one who entered the country where he is living without having gone through the established legal process for doing so. Substituting the term undocumented worker is an exercise in linguistic sleight-of-hand, the equivalent of calling a shoplifter "a non-paying customer." To paraphrase Shakespeare, you can call a rose by another name but it remains a rose.

Illegal is not a pretty word, but it accurately defines a situation in which a law is broken. Entering a country without fulfilling the requirements set by that country is as illegal as taking an item from a store without paying for it.

The law makes provision for people to come to this country and become citizens or, if they wish, simply to work or study for a time and then to return home. The process is orderly and fair. Of course, time and paperwork are involved but that is unavoidable. It is certainly not an excuse for people to flout the law.

The number of illegal aliens in the United States is estimated at between eight and thirteen million individuals. To be sure, most simply wish to pursue a better life. But some are criminals or terrorists who pose a threat to our citizens and our way of life.

A movement has arisen in this country to ignore or even approve illegal immigration. Supporters of that movement believe that people here illegally should be granted the same rights as those who honored the immigration laws and even the rights of citizenship, including voting rights. Some even would approve in-state tuition preferences. This would mean that an illegal immigrant in California would pay significantly less to attend college there than a U.S.-born citizen of Nevada or Oregon!

Despite their good intentions, people who approve illegal immigration are undermining our legal system, supporting the individuals engaged in smuggling in immigrants (many of whom are also drug smugglers), creating a burden on the American taxpayer, and threatening homeland security. Their efforts should be strongly opposed.

◢ Exercise 45 (cont.)

Send Me Your Poor
By Maria Maloney

To begin with, the term illegal alien is abhorrent. Illegal suggests that the person's existence is somehow suspect. And calling human beings "aliens" puts them in the same category as imaginary beings from another planet. That's offensive!

Let's be clear about this. This issue concerns flesh and blood people like you and me who have fled poverty or oppression in search of a better life. True, they didn't fill out all the forms required by the immigration bureaucracy and get the required visa, but that's not reason enough to imprison or deport them.

The vast majority of undocumented individuals in the United States are hardworking people. Not only are they willing to perform menial work that others won't do—many companies are eager to employ them. And here's another dirty secret: some of the politicians who shout the loudest about securing our borders conveniently ignore the immigration status of the nannies, maids, and gardeners they hire.

Debate about undocumented individuals often focuses on whether they are entitled to the rights enjoyed by U.S. citizens. Some writers have argued for denying them driver's licenses, voting rights, access to healthcare facilities, and education. That position is exclusionary, vindictive, and inhumane.

What makes a country great is not the size of its military arsenal, the extent of its natural resources, or the monetary wealth of its citizens. No, what makes a country great is the depth of its compassion towards the poor and needy. If America wishes to merit the title "great," it must accept all who reside within its borders regardless of how they happen to have arrived.

All Americans would do well to remember the words inscribed on our Statue of Liberty: "Give me your tired, your poor,/ Your huddled masses yearning to breathe free,/ The wretched refuse of your teeming shore./ Send these, the homeless, tempest-tossed to me,/ I lift my lamp beside the golden door!"

▶ Exercise 46

Analyze ONE of the following arguments using the five-step approach detailed in Chapter Four. In conducting your research, be especially careful to look for any errors in thinking and examine viewpoints that differ from the one presented.

DISPLAY THE TEN COMMANDMENTS

A. Let me make it clear at the outset that I am not insensitive to the feelings of religious minorities. My great-grandparents came to this country from Ireland as young children in the 1890s. They attended public schools in New York City. Their teachers often read from the King James (Protestant) Bible and even led the children in the recitation of the Protestant version of the Lord's Prayer. If Catholics (like my grandparents) or Jews objected, they were told to "get used to it." That wasn't acceptable then and it's not now.

Nevertheless, I am in favor of posting the Ten Commandments in every public school classroom in this country. Is this a contradiction? Not at all, because I favor posting other religious/moral codes alongside the Ten Commandments. Does that mean the Muslim, Buddhist, Hindu, and Native American equivalents of the Ten Commandments. Absolutely. The codes of atheistic or agnostic groups, such as Secular Humanists, too? Of course.

If this approach were taken, no students or parents would have reason to be offended. No one's beliefs would be excluded. No one would be given promi-nence. Some would argue that having no religious or moral codes on the wall is better than having many of them there. I say that the very purpose of the school is to lead students out of ignorance and into knowledge. Banishing all codes dig-nifies ignorance.

B. Religion has been among the most powerful forces in human history. So have moral codes. Putting reminders of both in prominent places in institutions of learning may not be a panacea. But if students happen to look at them, they might notice how similar most of them are. A few students might even get around to thinking about the connection between morality, law, and a safe society. I can think of worse things.

THE HIGH COST OF POLICING THE WORLD

No sensible person would deny that the U.S.-led attack on Iraq has benefited the people of that country. Saddam and his brutal followers were a cancer that needed to be excised. Unfortunately, the success of that operation is likely to embolden the militaristic-minded to see it as the model for dealing with problems in other countries, in other words, for the United States to become the police force of the world. Here are four good reasons for such thinking to be rejected.

First, for the United States to take on the role of the world's police force would divert attention from domestic problems. These include needed improvements in

▨▶ Exercise 46 (cont.)

public education, poverty, and joblessness in the inner city; homelessness and substance abuse; the destruction of the environment; and the limitations of present health insurance coverage.

Second, the use of U.S. troops in foreign policing operations would put them in harm's way. The nature of such operations puts restrictions on a soldier's ability to defend himself or herself. Whereas in military actions they can attack the enemy, in police actions they can only react, and even then may use only minimal force. Moreover, if members of the armed services are suitable in the role of police officers (a debatable matter), the place to use them is not in foreign lands but in the United States for the protection of our northern and southern borders.

Third, for the United States to police the world would place an immense financial burden on taxpayers. It is expensive enough to deploy troops in a single foreign campaign. The cost of doing so in many places at the same time would be prohibitive.

Fourth, if the United States assumed the role of police force to the world, the world's reaction would be to hate us even more than at present. The only thing worse than a meddler in other's affairs is an *armed* meddler. And that is just what we would be.

HOW THE MEDIA DISTORT REALITY

TV and movie apologists are forever telling us that we have no business criticizing them because they are only holding a mirror up to reality. Many people buy that explanation, but they shouldn't.

It would be more accurate to say the media hold a magnifying glass to carefully selected realities—namely, the most outrageous and sensational events of the day, such as the tragic deaths of John F. Kennedy Jr. and Princess Diana, or the trials of celebrities such as O. J. Simpson, Kobe Bryant, and Michael Jackson.

Consider how this happens. The first platoon of media people report the latest sensational story as it unfolds, squeezing each new development for all the airtime or newsprint it will yield. Meanwhile, agents and attorneys are negotiating the sale of movie and TV rights to the story. The sleazier the story, the greater the payoff. After the movie is produced, every situation comedy, detective show, and western drama builds an episode around the successful theme.

In this way a single despicable, disgusting act—real or imagined—can generate months of sensational media fare.

In short, the media exploit our social problems for ratings, feed us a steady diet of debasing material, celebrate irresponsible behavior, and then have the audacity to blame parents and teachers for the social problems that result.

☑ quiz

Write your answers on a separate sheet of paper.

1. Explain each of the following terms and describe how errors in the category affect the thinking process:

   Errors of perception

   Errors of judgment

   Errors of reaction

2. Define each of the following errors, and explain when it occurs in the thought process:

   Double standard

   Shifting the burden of proof

   Unwarranted assumption

   "Mine is better" thinking

   Gullibility and skepticism

   Irrelevant criterion

   Pretending to know

   Attacking the person

   Oversimplification

   Bias for or against change

☑ quiz (cont.)

Straw man

Explaining away

Selective perception

Hasty conclusion

Overgeneralizing or stereotyping

Failure to make a distinction

Bias

Either/or thinking

Answers to this quiz may be found at http://studentsuccess.college.hmco.com/ students.

CHAPTER 6

Applying Your Thinking Skills

IN THIS CHAPTER:

Thinking critically about

...everyday problems	*Solve unsatisfactory situations.*
...relationships	*Improve your relationships.*
...careers	*Make sensible career decisions.*
...ethical judgments	*Master the use of ethical criteria.*
...commercials	*Evaluate the impact of TV commercials.*
...print advertising	*Assess the quality and honesty of ads.*
...TV programming	*Determine the effects of TV on people.*
...movies	*Examine characters, plot, setting, and theme.*
...music	*Decide if popular music is antisocial.*
...magazines	*Decide whether the sensational is glorified.*
...newspapers	*Evaluate the views in editorials and letters.*
...the Internet	*Ask probing questions while online.*

145

Thinking critically about everyday problems

The scene is a Nazi concentration camp during World War II. A young boy is directed to the left, the death line. He follows the other prisoners into the special barracks that will house them until execution. There is only one door and that is guarded by armed soldiers. How can he possibly escape certain death?

Looking around the barracks, he spots a pail of water and a brush. He gets them, falls to his knees, and begins scrubbing the floor, slowly backing closer to the door. Then, still scrubbing, he backs his way out the door and down the steps.

At the bottom the boy stands and slowly walks away, pail in hand. Once across the yard, he mingles with a group of other prisoners. Though the guards have seen his every move, rather than question him they assume he was assigned to scrub the barracks.

This true story is recounted by the man it happened to, Samuel Pisar, in his book *Of Blood and Hope.* It illustrates the problem-solving process used every day in a variety of situations. Of course, most situations are less dramatic and urgent than this one. And most offer more time to find a solution.

Problem solving has a different objective than the thinking applications that have occupied our attention in previous chapters. The aim in problem solving is not to find the most reasonable viewpoint on a disputed issue but instead to find *the most effective solution to an unsatisfactory situation.*

For example, when Arthur Scott's company received a shipment of paper that was too heavy and wrinkled to be used for its bathroom tissue, his solution was to invent the paper towel. Similarly, when Dr. Henry Heimlich realized that the standard emergency response to choking was ineffective, he devised the now-famous "Heimlich maneuver."

And when Sky Dalton experienced difficulty configuring his computer for Internet use, he invented EarthLink. (In the first section of this book, "Strategies for Effective Learning," we noted several other examples of solutions to problems.)

Following is an approach that will help you become a more effective problem solver:

Step 1: Be alert for problems

You've probably heard the old saying, "If it isn't broken, don't fix it." That's good advice. And the corollary is equally important—*if it is broken, do fix it,* and do so as soon as possible. Many people prefer to ignore problems, hoping that they will go away. But neglected problems seldom go away. In fact, they often get bigger and bigger, until they reach the crisis stage and are more difficult and costly to solve.

The most reliable signal of a problem is a feeling of frustration, annoyance, or disappointment. Whenever you have such a feeling—or hear someone else complain of having one—scribble a brief note for later reference. A few key words should be enough to help you recall the problem later. For example, if you keep having difficulty finding a parking place on campus, you might write "parking: . . . argh!" If you serve on a committee with a pushy person, just write "dealing with Laura."

Once you resolve to be alert for problems, you will be surprised at how many you find. They are all around you, waiting to be recognized . . . and solved. There are problems with products, procedures, processes, and relationships. Some problems are personal, while others are societal, affecting not just one or a few people but entire communities and nations.

Step 2: Express the problem

"A problem well stated," observed Henry Hazlitt, "is half solved." He realized that each expression of a problem creates its own path toward solution. No two paths are exactly alike.

The societal problem of drunken driving, for example, might be expressed in any of the following ways, among others:

How can we most effectively *punish* drunken drivers?

How can we *educate* people about the effects of drunken driving?

How can we *persuade* people to take the car keys away from friends who have had too much to drink?

How can we *demonstrate* that alcohol seriously affects drivers' reflexes?

How can we *modify cars* so a drunken person can't operate them?

Notice that question 1 leads to ideas for punishment; question 2, to educational ideas; questions 3 and 4, to explanations or persuasive strategies; question 5, to modifications in cars rather than drivers. Which is the best expression? We can't say until after we have produced many ideas for each expression and evaluated all the ideas. This much, however, is clear—the question that focuses on punishment is not likely to produce ideas for education or for modifying cars. To omit any of these questions is to cheat yourself of possible solutions.

Step 3: List possible solutions

After asking many "how can" questions, brainstorm each question and think of as many possible answers as you can. This will produce a generous supply of possible solutions. Why is it important to produce many possible solutions? Because the first ones that come to mind are usually the most familiar and common ones, the ones that have been tried and found to be unsatisfactory. To be an effective problem solver, you must get beyond these. Here are five proven ways of doing so:

1. After listing the common, familiar solutions, list as many new and different possibilities as you can, ones you've never heard before.

2. Read your list of solutions aloud and think of as many additional associations as you can.

3. Examine the problem again and ask what it reminds you of. Where appropriate, also ask what it looks, sounds, or functions like. These questions will often produce analogies that stimulate idea production.

4. Consider combining two or more possible solutions in an unusual way.

5. Try to visualize what the situation would be like if the problem were overcome and study that image for clues to the solution.

While you are taking these steps, resist the temptation to analyze each idea as it comes to you. Doing so interrupts the flow of ideas and may result in your rejecting a creative idea simply because it is unfamiliar. Postpone all evaluation until you have completed your list of possible solutions. Remember that the more ideas you produce, the better your chance of producing a really good one.

Step 4: Select and refine your best solution

When you have extended your effort and identified many possible solutions, review your list and choose the two or three solutions that seem most promising. For each of those solutions, answer the following questions:

When, where, and by whom would it be carried out?

How would it be accomplished, step by step?

How would it be financed?

What additional people, materials, and equipment, if any, would be required?

What changes would this solution necessitate?

What objections might be raised about this solution? Consider legal, moral, safety, and financial objections, as well as those concerning ease of implementation.

The answers to these questions will help you decide which of the two or three promising solution is most effective and practical. Then refine that solution to overcome any reasonable objections to it.

Exercise 47

List all the situations, processes, procedures, and implementations that have caused you annoyance, aggravation, or frustration recently. Add to this list the complaints your have heard others make about such things.

____

____

____

____

____

Exercise 48

Select one of the items you listed in the previous exercise and apply the problem-solving approach explained in this section. Record all your thoughts. (If the space provided is insufficient, continue your work on a separate sheet of paper.)

_____

_____

_____

_____

_____

Exercise 49

Changes are often made in the rules and procedures of sports. Choose your favorite sport and imagine you are a member of the rules committee considering how to make the sport more challenging or exciting to play, as well as more enjoyable to watch. Apply the problem-solving approach explained in this section. Use a separate sheet of paper for this exercise.

Exercise 50

Two main causes of divorce are carelessness in selecting a marriage partner and ignorance of the demands of marriage and parenthood. In many cases, the home, the school, and the church are not meeting the challenge of preparing young people for marriage. Treat this situation as a problem and solve it on a separate sheet of paper, using the problem-solving approach explained in this section. Use a separate sheet of paper for this exercise.

Thinking critically about relationships

A relationship is a significant association between or among people. Relationships differ in intensity. You may visit your bank, grocery store, and post office at least once a week, yet your relationship with the people who work there is probably casual, at best. On the other hand, your relationships with old friends and former classmates are no doubt much deeper,

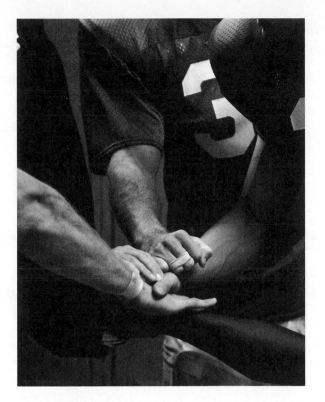

even though you may see them only once or twice a year. Generally speaking, the most significant relationships are *teaching/learning, business, family,* and *personal* relationships. (The personal category includes both friendships and romantic/marital relationships.)

In recent years, much has been written about "dysfunctional" relationships. Dysfunctional is a fancy word for "troubled." The number of troubled relationships seems to be increasing, and if that is the case, a likely reason is that self-help books, articles, and tapes have emphasized putting self above others. They urge us to "look out for number one," to be assertive about our rights, and to resist being taken advantage of by others.

Such advice contains an element of truth. It is possible to be so concerned about other people that we do ourselves a disservice. Some individuals give up their own hopes and dreams in order to please a selfish, overly demanding parent. Others allow themselves to be taken advantage of by their children or shamelessly overworked, underpaid, and even harassed by their employers. In such cases, the advice to stand up for oneself is good advice. But that advice is definitely not appropriate for people who are so absorbed in themselves and their rights that they ignore other people's rights. Such people need to give *less attention to asserting their rights and more to accepting their responsibilities.*

Responsibility is an important ingredient in relationships. For example, teachers are responsible for making lessons clear and challenging, offering constructive criticism, and testing and grading fairly. Students, in turn, are responsible for completing assignments on time, paying attention in class, and accepting criticism graciously and thoughtfully. Similarly, friends and family members have the *mutual* responsibility of giving support, encouragement, and loyalty, as well as consolation in times of sorrow.

▶ # Good Thinking!

The Story of Aaron Feuerstein

Suppose you were the 70-year-old owner of a large textile plant with 3,200 employees and you woke one morning to discover that the entire plant had been destroyed by fire. What would you do? Many would lay off the employees, take the insurance money, and retire. There would be nothing morally wrong with that response. With no factory you would have no work for the employees to do, and at age 70 it would be perfectly reasonable to retire.

That was not Aaron Feuerstein's response when his company, Malden Mills, burned down in December 1995. Best known for its Polartec fabric, the company had been in the family since his grandfather had established it in the early 1900s. And Feuerstein had a very different attitude from the one that has become so common in modern business. A deeply religious man, he felt a responsibility to his employees and to the town of Methuen where the plant was located.

So Aaron Feuerstein kept all the employees on the payroll for three months and even gave them a Christmas bonus, all out of his own pocket, for an estimated cost of $15 million. And then he set about rebuilding the business. In four months the plant was back in production and the world knew of his generosity. He had not sought publicity, but the press had searched him out to ask why he had performed such amazing acts of kindness. His reply was simple and direct: "It was the right thing to do."

Later, in a presentation at MIT, Feuerstein reflected on what had gone through his mind immediately after the fire: "I had to rebuild. There was no way I was going to take 3,000 people and throw them in the streets. And there was no way that I should be the one to condemn that community, which had suffered so much in the twentieth century, to economic oblivion. No sir."

In a time when the "bottom line" often seems to be the centerpiece of corporate philosophy, Aaron Feuerstein's moral guideline of doing the right thing seems hopelessly outdated. But it shines as brightly as ever.

For more information on Aaron Feuerstein, see www.geocities.com/Yosemite/Trails/9426/day5.html or www.compassionatework.com/art_malden_mills.html.

Guidelines for Successful Relationships

Good relationships are not the result of chance or fortune—they are created and maintained by observing some basic guidelines. In Chapter Two you encountered the most general and basic of these guidelines, the Golden Rule: "Do unto others as you would have them do unto you." Following are more specific guidelines that flow from this rule:

1. *Acknowledge other people.* Many people are so absorbed in their thoughts that they ignore others. When you pass someone on campus that you recognize from one of your classes, make eye contact, smile, and where appropriate, offer a greeting. Do the same for the mail carrier, the waiter or waitress in a restaurant, and others with whom you have some transaction. As Frederick W. Faber wisely observed, "Many a friendship, long, loyal, and self-sacrificing, rested at first on no thicker a foundation than a kind word."

2. *Be generous with compliments, stingy with criticism and/or advice.* People like receiving compliments and are generally grateful to receive them, provided they are sincere. Similarly, most people resent unsolicited advice. Never give unsolicited advice. Even when advice is asked for, try to determine whether the person really wants it. If the person seems to want approval that you cannot, in honesty, give, say this: "I sense that you'd like me to say _____. But I really don't think that is the best response. I'll be glad to explain why if you'd like."

3. *Keep your moods to yourself.* No one likes to be in the company of people who are forever moaning or complaining. Make a special effort to be positive and upbeat in your remarks.

4. *Expect more of yourself and less of others.* The more you expect of others, the more you will be tempted to criticize them for their shortcomings. By setting higher expectations for yourself than for others, you will be more inclined to focus on improving *yourself.* This habit will help you to grow and develop as a person and make you more pleasant to be around. Moreover, your good example to others will be more persuasive than any lecture could be.

5. *Make allowance for differences of opinion.* Whenever you discuss controversial matters—for example, social, religious, or political issues—try to present your views clearly, not to change people's minds. If you aim for the latter, you will usually be disappointed.

6. *Be sensitive to others' feelings.* This rule can be difficult to observe because rudeness has become fashionable. We see it in homes and schools, in offices and grocery stores, on the telephone and in Internet chat rooms, at airports and on the highways. Crude and

disrespectful language and behavior are also modeled in modern entertainment, including rap music, TV situation comedies, and "reality" programming. Resist these negative influences and avoid words and gestures that insult, ridicule, or humiliate others, even jokingly. (The targets of such humor may join in the laughter yet still, at a deeper level, be offended.)

7. *Balance talking with listening.* There is no shortage of excellent talkers, but excellent listeners are rare, and therefore greatly appreciated. You'll also learn a great deal more by listening than by talking.

8. *Think before speaking.* Blurting out whatever happens to pop into your mind is a sure way to cause problems in your relationships. In contrast, pausing to ask yourself, "What effect will saying this have? Should I say it at all, and if so, how should I phrase it?" is a sure way to avoid problems.

9. *Purge negative emotions.* Negative emotions have a way of becoming visible to other people and disrupting relationships. If they remain hidden, they can be unhealthy for you. Whenever negative emotions arise, talk yourself out of them. This will be difficult to do when they represent a response to a real offense or provocation. But even in that case, make the effort.

10. *Refrain from gossiping.* Talking about others behind their backs is a sign of disrespect for them and could easily damage a relationship. Keep in mind, too, that whoever is willing to gossip to you about someone else is just as likely to talk to someone else about *you!* André Maurois writes of a woman with a perfect approach to such situations. He explained that "whenever one of her intimates is attacked in her presence, [she] merely states: 'She is my friend,' and refuses to say more."

11. *Apologize when you are wrong.* Few expressions have the healing power of "I'm sorry." These words have been known to eradicate generations of animosity and resentment and restore relationships that were thought to be irreparable. Unfortunately, the longer you wait to say these words, the harder it is to say them. Develop the habit of saying them as soon as you realize you were wrong. And if you feel you were only partly wrong, apologize for that part.

12. *Forgive when you are wronged.* Forgiving others can be even more difficult than apologizing, particularly if the other person has not apologized for having wronged you. But without forgiveness, resentments remain, prevent relationships from healing,

and harm you. A character in Mitch Albom's novel *The Five People You Meet in Heaven* explains why: "Holding anger is a poison. It eats you from inside. We think that hating is a weapon that attacks the person who harmed us. But hatred is a curved blade. And the harm we do, we do to ourselves" (Albom, 141).

13. *Be a peacemaker.* When people you know and care about are having difficulties in their relationships, and one or both discuss the problem with you, it is often difficult to know what to say. The wrong words may worsen the situation and even cause one or both people to resent you. If you can't say something that will promote understanding and healing, say only "I care about both of you and I hope you find a way to restore your relationship."

14. *Meet your responsibilities to others.* In all your relationships, be aware of your obligations to the other people and do your best to meet those obligations.

15. *Look for opportunities to be kind.* To be worthy of the greatest respect from those around you, follow Charles Kingsley's advice and live each day in such a way that when you close your eyes at night you can honestly say, "I have made one human being at least a little wiser, a little happier or a little better this day."

⏩ Exercise 51

Review the fifteen guidelines for successful relationships and list the ones which you are in the habit of observing and the ones on which you still need to work.

_____

_____

_____

_____

_____

_____

▟ Exercise 52

Consider your most significant *teaching/learning* or *business* (that is, employer/employee) relationships and decide which one is *least* successful. Describe what is wrong with that relationship and explain which of the guidelines for successful relationships can help to improve it. (Note: In some situations, several rules will apply.)

_____

_____

_____

_____

_____

_____

▟ Exercise 53

Consider your most significant *family* or *personal* relationships and decide which one is *least* successful. Describe what is wrong with that relationship and explain which of the guidelines for successful relationships can help to improve it. (Note: In some situations, several rules will apply.)

_____

_____

_____

_____

_____

_____

Thinking critically about careers

The choice of a career is one of the most important decisions you will ever make. The reason is fairly obvious. If you are like most people, you will work eight hours a day, five days a week, forty-eight weeks a year, for forty or more years. That adds up to almost 77,000 hours of your life. A wise career choice will ensure that most of those hours will be satisfying and fulfilling. A foolish choice could mean self-inflicted misery.

Given this reality, it is astounding how many people put little more thought into choosing a career than they would into choosing a video game or a music CD. Some decide on the tasks or level of remuneration they imagine to be associated with various careers: "Lawyers deal with interesting cases and make lots of money, so I guess I'll be a lawyer." Others choose on the basis of some personal preference: "I love animals, so I'll be a veterinarian," or "I like to help people, so I'll be a social worker," or "I love food, so I'll be a chef."

These approaches to choosing a career are unrealistic for several reasons:

- The tasks or level of remuneration associated with a career may not be as you imagine.
- Merely loving something about a field may not qualify you for candidacy in a program of studies. You may also need to demonstrate, through academic achievement or in some other way, that you have certain aptitudes or skills.
- The occupation may involve more or different tasks than you are aware of. And some of them you may find boring or unfulfilling.
- The job market in the field may be poor. Thus, after devoting many years to formal education and incurring tens of thousands of dollars in expense, you may not be able to find employment in the field.

The practice of law is seldom as glamorous as courtroom dramas make it seem. Many lawyers spend little, if any, time in the courtroom; their jobs consist mostly of working with legal documents such as contracts. And even courtroom lawyers spend more time poring over law books than questioning witnesses or delivering dramatic summations to juries. In addition, the preparation to be a lawyer is long and demanding—four years of college, followed by the rigors of law school.

Numerous careers associated with law, such as police officer, court reporter, and paralegal, require considerably less preparation. One could also be a journalist specializing in legal matters.

Not everyone who loves animals can meet the science requirements for veterinary medicine. Even those who can meet them may have difficulty gaining acceptance to a veterinary science program because relatively few colleges offer that specialty. Yet there are many other careers that people who love animals might consider—for example, animal trainer, animal breeder, or veterinary technician.

Similarly, someone who likes to help people has many more career choices than social worker, including nurse, guidance counselor, and occupational therapist. And someone who loves food should not limit his or her focus to the career of chef but also consider other food-related careers, such as nutritionist or restaurant manager, or a position in the sales or marketing division of a food company.

A sensible approach

The most sensible approach to choosing a career is to assess your interests, identify some broad career areas that seem suited to your aptitudes and skills, and then investigate those areas and decide which you should consider.

The best starting point for your investigation into career possibilities is your campus career center. Peter Vogt of MonsterTRAK.com, the college division of the career website Monster.com, offers seven reasons for becoming acquainted with your campus career center (www.quintcareers. com/campus_career_centers.html/; used with permission).

1. "It's staffed by professionals who are *specifically* trained to assist college students with career-related concerns.

2. "Its staff members work closely with the employers who will some-day hire you.

3. "It's the best place on campus to help you figure out what you want to do with your life and how.

4. "It's loaded with career-related resources, whether in print or on the computer.

5. "The more "known" you are to the career services staff, the better the chance a staffer will refer you to an employer looking to fill a specific position.

6. "It's a good place to meet other students who share your worries.

7. "You're [already] paying for it!"

A number of Internet websites are also available to assist you in your investigation into career possibilities. The standard reference is the

Occupational Outlook Handbook published by the U. S. Department of Labor, Bureau of Labor Statistics. The Internet address is www.bls.gov/oco/home.htm.

Another helpful resource is the Minnesota Careers website at www.mncareers.org. The interest-assessment test offered there will reveal which one (or combination) of the following descriptions fits you best: *Realistic, Investigative, Artistic, Social, Enterprising,* or *Conventional.* A list of occupations for each description is also provided. For each occupation, there is information about the kind of work you would do, the educational background required, the salary range, and the job outlook.

Yet another helpful site is the College of St. Catherine's Career Development website at http://minerva.stkate.edu/careers.nsf/pages/selfassmnt_rsrcs#interest. This site provides links to a number of interest-assessment tools, including the Minnesota Careers site and the Princeton Review Career quiz site. (Note: The "Career Briefs" link is also very useful.)

To find other, related websites, go to Google and use the search term "personal interest assessment."

Thinking critically about ethical judgments*

Ethical judgments, also known as moral judgments, are the decisions people make about the rightness or wrongness of human behavior. Over the last century, considerable disagreement has arisen about the basis of such judgments. Some say the basis is each person's feelings: in other words, if someone feels a certain action is morally acceptable, then it is acceptable, at least for that person. In theory, this view sounds reasonable. But would it prove to be so when applied to actual events?

▰▶ Exercise 54

Visit your campus Career Center and ask for an explanation of the various services provided there. Then in the space below record what you learned and the name of the person you spoke to.

_____

_____

_____

_____

_____

---

* For a more detailed treatment of this subject, see Vincent Ryan Ruggiero, *Thinking Critically About Ethical Issues,* 6th ed. (New York: McGraw-Hill, 2004).

▶ Exercise 55

Visit the U. S. Department of Labor website and examine the *Occupational Outlook Handbook*. Begin by checking the "search tips" in the middle of the home page. Then examine the various features and record your findings in the space provided.

_____

_____

_____

_____

_____

▶ Exercise 56

Visit the Minnesota Careers website, take the interest-assessment test, and read the information about the occupations associated with your descriptive term. Record your findings in the space provided.

_____

_____

_____

_____

_____

▶ Exercise 57

Visit the College of St. Catherine's Career Development website and explore the various links, including the "Career Briefs" link. Decide which of the links are most useful to you. Explain your findings in the space provided.

_____

_____

_____

_____

_____

⏩ Exercise 58

Visit Google and conduct a search using the search term "personal interest assessment." Sample at least three of your findings and decide how useful they are. Describe each below and explain your assessment of each.

_____

_____

_____

_____

_____

_____

In the late 1930s and early 1940s, on the orders of their leader Adolph Hitler, the Nazis killed nine million people. Most of the victims were Jews, gypsies, and physically or mentally compromised individuals, all of whom the Nazis classified as "life unworthy of life." The Nazis felt these killings were morally acceptable.

Before 1964 many U.S. restaurant owners had a policy of serving only white people. The same was true of many hotel, motel, and theater owners. These owners felt that the policy was morally acceptable—in fact, some believed that to allow "non-whites" to mingle with white people in their establishments would have been morally wrong.

To say that the Nazis' feelings and the establishment owners' feelings justified their actions is _to ignore the feelings of the people hurt by their_

actions, and that is irresponsible. That is precisely why an international court found the Nazis guilty of "crimes against humanity" and the Civil Rights Act of 1964 required the owners of establishments that serve the public to treat all patrons equally.

Many similar examples could be cited. Robbery, sexual harassment, spouse abuse, rape, child molestation, and murder may be prompted by powerful feelings, urges, and impulses. Nevertheless, they harm others and violate their rights. That is why they are against the law.

A Better Basis for Judgment

Clearly, we need a better basis for ethical judgment than our feelings. But what, exactly, should that basis be? Let's begin by noting that all the offenses noted in the above examples have one thing in common—they violate people's rights.

This theme of rights is found in many important documents. For example, the U.S. Declaration of Independence declares that "all Men are created equal, and they are endowed by their Creator with certain unalienable rights, that among these are Life, Liberty, and the Pursuit of Happiness." The United Nations Declaration of Human Rights claims that "human rights should be protected by the rule of law." Similarly, medical associations' codes of ethics speak of patients' rights; legal codes of ethics affirm clients' rights; and corporate codes of ethics acknowledge the rights of employees and customers.

Such acknowledgement of the rights of individuals is referred to in ethics as the *principle of respect for persons*. According to Errol E. Harris, the principle incorporates several requirements:

> First, that each and every person should be regarded as worthy of sympathetic consideration, and should be so treated; secondly, that no person should be regarded as a mere possession, or used as a mere instrument, or treated as a mere obstacle, to another's satisfaction; and thirdly, that persons are not and ought never to be treated in any undertaking as mere expendables (Harris, "Respect for Persons, *Dædalus,* Spring 1969, 113).

Over the centuries ethicists have identified three criteria helpful in deciding when actions honor the principle of respect for persons and when they do not. The three criteria are *obligations, moral ideals,* and *consequences.* Let's look more closely at each:

Obligations. Human relationships create various kinds of obligations, all of which place requirements or restrictions on people's behavior. Contractual obligations require people to honor whatever terms they have agreed to honor. Employment obligations make demands on both employers and employees. Professional obligations require that clients' or patients' interests be served. Obligations of friendship demand mutual support, encouragement, and the keeping of confidences. Marital obligations demand mutual love and honor and faithful devotion in sickness and in health.

Moral ideals. Moral ideals, also known as virtues, are standards of excellence in behavior. There are many such ideals, the best known of which are justice, fairness, and honesty. Other important ideals include kindness, compassion, and forgiveness.

Consequences. This is the broadest of the criteria for making ethical judgments. All actions produce consequences. Some consequences are positive, others negative. Some impact the person who takes the action, others the people who are acted upon. (The effects may be physical, emotional, spiritual, social, and/or economic.) Similarly, some consequences occur immediately, whereas others are delayed for months and even years.

▶ Good Thinking!

The Story of Chiara Lubich

When the bombs were dropping on her native Trent in Italy during World War II, young Chiara Lubich and her companions sat huddled in bomb shelters reading the Gospel. Certain phrases had special meaning for them, especially "Love one another as I have loved you." They decided that love is supposed to be *lived*, and not just talked about. Thus began the Focolare ("hearth") Movement. The name is apt, for this movement warms and nurtures the cause of brotherhood.

The movement's main focus is the "spirituality of unity." Members combine passion for their own religious beliefs with deep respect for people of different beliefs and no beliefs. The movement has developed dialog relationships not only with the members of the various Christian denominations, but also with Jews, Buddhists, Muslims, and Hindus, as well as agnostics and atheists.

These relationships go far beyond listening politely to one another. They aim at discovering common values and finding ways to express those values together.

The Focolare Movement has established little towns that serve as "models for a new humanity." There are twenty such towns and they are found on every continent. The people who live and visit there subscribe to the "law of reciprocal love."

In Brazil and Argentina the movement developed an economic system known as "the economy of sharing." In this system, participating businesses use one-third of their profits for capital reinvestment, one-third to raise the standard of living of the less privileged, and one-third for structures such as community centers in which the values of sharing and harmonious living are taught. More than 700 businesses are now participating in those and other countries.

In 1977 Chiara Lubich was awarded the Templeton Prize for Progress in Religion.

For more information on Chiara Lubich, see www.rc.net/focolare/chiara.htm.

Applying the criteria

The three criteria provide a sound basis for deciding whether an action is ethical. Here is how to proceed:

Step 1: Examine the situation and determine the obligations, if any, that exist; the moral ideals that are relevant; and the people who are likely to be affected by whatever action is taken.

Step 2: Determine the various actions that could be taken and the various consequences—subtle as well as obvious, long-term as well as immediate—that each action would likely have on the people involved. *Caution: Be sure to consider all possible actions and not just the one you prefer. Also, resist the temptation to ignore unpleasant consequences.*

Step 3: Decide which action honors the obligations and the moral ideals and produces the most desirable consequences for the various people involved. In cases where a conflict exists between two obligations, two ideals, or an obligation and an ideal, decide which is the more important. Also, when you must choose between two good actions, choose the one that represents the greater good. Similarly, when your only choice is between two harmful actions, choose the one that does less harm.

A sample case

Luke, a senior journalism student, is facing a dilemma. Earlier this term, his final semester, he was given the major assignment of doing a feature story on an interesting person of his choosing. The assignment is due tomorrow. However, he hasn't yet decided whom to interview, let alone conducted the interview and written the story. (One reason is that he has been busy with his work in other courses; another, more significant reason is that he is socially hyperactive.)

Luke could ask his instructor for extra time but he knows that there will be a penalty of at least one letter grade, possibly two, and he is barely passing now. Moreover, if he were to repeat the course, he could not graduate until the following year because the course is offered only in the spring semester. For these reasons, Luke is considering two alternatives. One is to search the Internet, find an obscure but well-written feature article, and, after making strategic changes to disguise it, submit it as his own. The other alternative is to create an imaginary person, conduct an imaginary interview, and write a bogus feature story. Given the difficulty of Luke's situation, would either of these alternative approaches be ethical? Let's apply the criteria and see:

Step 1: Luke has the obligation to do the work assigned to him and to submit it on time. The relevant ideal is honesty, which in this case prohibits both plagiarizing someone else's work and passing fiction off as fact.

Step 2: The most obvious action would be for Luke to present his case to the instructor and hope for a lenient penalty. One clear consequence is that he could take satisfaction in his honesty and willingness to accept responsibility for his laziness. Beyond that, the consequences are uncertain. He could receive a low passing grade and graduate on time, or he could fail the course and have to wait until next year to graduate.

One alternative would be for Luke to submit the article he found on the Internet as his own. If his deception were successful, he would graduate on time; however, if the instructor discovered the plagiarism, Luke might fail the course and even (depending on the college's conduct code) be expelled.

Another alternative would be for Luke to create an imaginary person and write a bogus feature story. This deception is more likely to fool the instructor than the previous one. However, the consequence of this action is that it might tempt Luke to adopt it as a strategy for meeting deadlines after he graduates and is working as a journalist. And if he gave in to that temptation, he would run the risk of ruining his career. (If this seems overly dramatic, be assured that it is not. In recent years, a number of journalists have suffered professional disgrace when their dishonesty was discovered.)

Step 3: In this case, the ethical judgment is clear: both plagiarizing and creating a bogus story are unethical responses to the situation. Although we might *understand* how a weak person might choose one of these responses, there is no way to justify either response ethically.

Exercise 59

Select one of the following ethical issues and examine it using the three step approach for evaluating ethical issues. Record all your work on a separate sheet of paper.

A

Harry and Ruth are a financially successful married couple aged 53 and 50, respectively. Harry is the president of his own company. Once a fashion designer, Ruth no longer works but maintains an active social schedule. They live in a large house on Lake Michigan in suburban Chicago. Recently, Ruth's 80-year-old mother, Angela, suffered a fall in her modest apartment, where she had lived alone for the last ten years since her husband died. Because Angela suffers from osteoporosis, the doctors recommended that she no longer live alone. As an only child, Ruth had to decide whether to let her mother move into her home or move her to an assisted living facility. After talking the situation over with Harry, Ruth decided on the assisted living facility.

B

Lawrence Preston is a first-term congressman. The theme of the campaign that got him elected was to take government out of the hands of the special interest groups and return it to the people. Since taking office, however, he has been under considerable pressure from several special interest groups to endorse bills he believes are against the best interests of his constituents. He has asked two senior members of his party for their advice and they said: "Look at it this way, Larry. In order to represent your constituents' interests, you've got to stay in office. And you'll never get re-elected without the support of the special interest groups. So you'd better do as they say for a while. Postpone being a hero for a few terms." He decides to take their advice.

C

Ramona is a 35-year-old police woman who looks no older than 25. Her latest assignment is to go undercover and pose as a student at a university because the police suspect that a major drug operation is being run there. After a month on the job, she has made a number of friends among the students and faculty. Though she has no evidence that any of them are involved in the drug operation, she begins to feel guilty about not being able to be honest with them. Is it morally acceptable for her to continue on the assignment?

⯮ Exercise 60

Find an ethical issue currently being discussed on campus. Analyze the issue, using the three-step approach for evaluating ethical issues. Detail your findings below.

_____

_____

_____

_____

_____

_____

Thinking critically about commercials

Advertisers spend billions of dollars a year on commercials. The cost of just one 15-second commercial can exceed $500,000. In many cases advertising goes beyond presenting the product or service. Advertisers stimulate viewers through appeals to desires: to be youthful, sexually appealing, successful, loved, or accepted by others. In advertising language, the aim is to "sell the sizzle, not the steak."

In *Four Arguments for the Elimination of Television*, former advertising executive Jerry Mander claims that advertising exists only to create needs for products. The trick, he says, is to make people feel discontented. And the standard advertising formula for doing so is to (1) gain the audience's attention, (2) arouse their interest, (3) stimulate a desire for the product, and (4) make the sales pitch.

The design of a commercial (or print ad), Mander explains, is no casual affair. Advertisers employ thousands of psychologists, behavioral scientists, perception researchers, and sociologists. These experts identify deep-seated human needs and desires, insecurities and fears. Then they determine how these can be used to the advertiser's advantage. The most basic appeals are:

1. *Self-indulgence.* The appeal here is, "Don't deny yourself this [product or service]. Go ahead and treat yourself. You deserve it."

2. *Impulsiveness.* This appeal is "Don't delay. Don't pause to think and evaluate. Just act."

3. *Instant gratification.* The appeal here is "Why wait? You can enjoy it now and it will make you feel s-o-o-o-o good."

The techniques of advertising are the techniques of propaganda. Among the most common are the following:

Bandwagon
This technique creates the impression that everyone is buying the product or service. It appeals to the viewer's urge to conform.

Glittering generality
Here the advertiser uses words and phrases to imply excellence and uniqueness. Few specifics are offered. "Amazing new discovery," "now a stunning breakthrough," and "unheard-of softness" are examples of glittering generality.

Empty comparison
This technique uses words such as *better, bigger,* and *more* (as in "more economical") without completing the comparison. What, for example, does "greater cleaning power" mean? Greater than last year? Greater than the competition? Such a statement seems to make a serious claim. And yet we can't hold the advertiser responsible for it because we aren't sure just what is being claimed.

Meaningless slogan
Most large companies have slogans designed to create a positive impression. These create pleasant images but promise little.

United Airlines' slogan, "Fly the friendly skies," was designed to associate that airline with friendliness. "AT&T—The Right Choice" tried to link the act of choosing a telephone company with AT&T. Another slogan is "Michelin . . . because so much is riding on your tires," and with these words we see pictures of adorable babies. The aim: to have viewers associate buying Michelin tires with protecting their children.

Testimonial

A testimonial is an endorsement for a product or a service. Actors, musicians, sports figures, and other well-known people are paid substantial sums of money to appear in commercials, lending their credibility and celebrity status to products. The words they speak may be written by someone else, and viewers often know this. Even so, advertisers still hope we'll associate the celebrity with the product or service.

Transfer

One common kind of transfer is the voice-over. Here the celebrity never appears in the commercial but acts as off-camera narrator. Even if the viewer cannot name the speaker, the voice may be familiar and make the message more appealing.

Another kind of transfer involves objects instead of people. For example, the Statue of Liberty or the flag could be shown with a product or service. These symbols arouse strong positive feelings in many people. Advertisers want viewers to transfer those feelings to the product.

A less obvious use of transfer is the "party scene," in which we see people enjoying themselves. The intended message is that the featured product—a beer or wine cooler—made the occasion enjoyable.

Stacking the deck

We noted this technique in our discussion of manipulation in Chapter Three. This technique is also commonly used in advertising when comparisons are made between the advertiser's product and a competitor's product. For example, one commercial showed a competitor's fish sticks on a cookie sheet, all in black and white, looking as if they were still frozen. Then the scene shifted to the advertiser's frozen dinner appetizingly presented in vibrant color, with steam rising.

A similar approach is used in many diet commercials. For example, a "before" picture will be a fuzzy black and white print, with the person dressed poorly and looking sad. In contrast, the "after" picture will be sharply focused, in color, and with the person well dressed and happy.

Misleading statement

This technique uses words that invite viewers to make an erroneous interpretation. Such statements appear to promise something but in reality do not. Lately a number of long distance telephone ads use such statements.

One such commercial promises "Eight cents a minute for calls over ten minutes. That's a 50 percent saving." That invites thinkers to conclude that they will save 50 percent on every call. But the ad does not say what calls under ten minutes cost. Is it eight cents? Eighteen cents? Twenty-eight cents? We can't be sure.

Another commercial says we can talk up to twenty minutes for ninety-nine cents. We're tempted to think that's a rate of less than five cents a minute. But wait. If the ninety-nine cents is a flat rate, then a five-minute call would cost almost twenty cents a minute and a two-minute call would cost almost fifty cents! That's quite a difference.

The standard commercial break consists of four 15-second commercials. The average number of commercials in an hour of television viewing is forty-four. If you watch four hours of television a day you encounter 176 appeals designed to short-circuit your critical thinking and create an artificial desire or need. Your best safeguard against this manipulation is to use your critical thinking skills.

⬆️ Exercise 61

Watch at least two hours of television. Pay close attention to the commercials. For this assignment the programs themselves are unimportant. If you wish, do some other activity between commercial breaks. Or tape the program first.

As you observe each commercial, note the product or service advertised, the scenes shown, and the people on camera. Also listen for the narrator, music, and other sounds.

Next, select three of the commercials you observed. On a separate sheet of paper, describe each commercial and then analyze it by answering the following questions:

- Does the commercial motivate the viewers to think or merely appeal to their emotions? Explain.
- What hopes, fears, or desires is the commercial designed to exploit? How?
- What attitudes and values does the commercial promote—for example, attitudes about success and happiness? How does the commercial promote them? Do you share these attitudes and values?
- Does the commercial use propaganda techniques? How?
- Would you classify this commercial as fair or unfair persuasion? What's the evidence for your view?

▱ Exercise 62

Calculate the average attention shifts occurring during commercials. Proceed as follows, doing all your work on a separate sheet of paper:
1. Watch any half-hour or hour program. When a commercial break occurs, keep your eyes focused on the television set. Each time a new image appears on the screen, make a tally on the page. (Use a separate sheet of paper for this tally.) When the next commercial appears, resume your tally on a new line.
2. At the end of the program, divide the number of lines (that is, the number of commercials) into the grand total of stroke tallies. The answer will be the average attention shifts occurring during commercials for that program. Record your findings.
3. Comment on your findings. Were you surprised at the number of attention shifts per commercial? Explain. What possible reasons might advertising agencies have for changing images at that rate? Which of those reasons seems most likely? Explain.

▱ Exercise 63

This exercise extends the analysis of commercials you did in the previous exercise. Television commercials in the 1950s and 1960s were one minute long and contained relatively few images. Typically, one or more people talked about the product as they displayed it. In the 1970s and 1980s commercials were thirty seconds long and contained more images. Today's commercials are fifteen seconds in length and contain considerably more images. What effect, if any, could this change have had on academic performance? Job performance? Personal relationships? Explain your thoughts carefully.

_____

_____

_____

_____

_____

_____

⏩ Exercise 64

If you watch television, you've probably encountered some or all of the commercial slogans shown below. Reflect on them and decide if any of them are in any way objectionable. For each one you object to, write a brief explanation of your reaction. Use a separate sheet of paper for this exercise.

"Just do it." (Nike slogan)

"Image is everything." (Canon slogan)

"Life is short—play hard." (Reebok slogan)

"On planet Reebok there are no rules."

"Why ask why? Try Bud Dry." (Budweiser slogan)

Voice asks, "What should I drink?" Narrator says, "Give your brain a rest. Try some Sprite."

"Though we carry over 160,000 passengers a day, we serve each of them one at a time." (USAirways slogan)

"Red Wolf is here. Follow your instincts." (Red Wolf beer slogan)

"We measure success one investor at a time." (Dean Witter slogan)

Thinking critically about print advertising

Like television commercials, print advertising is designed to sell a product, a service, or an idea. Such advertising may appeal to the desire for happiness or the need for belonging, acceptance, or love. However, the techniques that print ads use are more limited. They cannot use sound or depict motion. They are strictly visual and static.

Advertisers know how to make a print ad effective. Every detail must contribute to the overall message. They take great care in choosing every word and picture.

Analyzing print ads involves studying these choices.

Always ask yourself whether the statements made in print ads make sense. Suppose an auto ad says, "Due to unprecedented demand, we are discounting hundreds of cars in our lot." But think about it. If the demand were high, the prices wouldn't be changed. The reality must be that *too few people* are buying.

Also read the fine print. No doubt you've gotten more than one credit card ad that says: "Why pay an adjustable rate of 17.9 percent or 18.9 percent when you can pay a low FIXED rate of only 4.9 percent?"

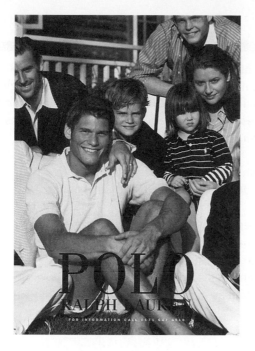

That certainly sounds like a great deal . . . until you look at the fine print and learn that the rate is "fixed" for three months. And after that? Presumably the sky's the limit.

Look critically at the pictures in print ads, too. Their effect can be even more powerful than words. Cigarette ads have been especially clever in depicting smokers as physically attractive people having a wonderful time as they puff.

Other ads are equally clever. A perfume ad pictured a man and a woman in a highly aroused state. The caption read, "Unleash your fantasies." The unspoken promise was that using the perfume would heighten sexual fulfillment.

Some ads are truly offensive. Another perfume ad showed a beautiful but frightened woman with several men clinging to her. The caption read "No one could protect her from herself." And a jeans ad showed a woman being backed into a fence by cowboys. The implied meaning of these ads was that women enjoy being assaulted.

Some critics say most advertising is dishonest at best. They are especially troubled by the ads directed at the most vulnerable individuals, children. Defenders of advertising deny the charge, claiming that advertising is simply honest persuasion.

⬛ Exercise 65

Visit the magazine section of your campus library. Skim at least a half-dozen magazines, looking for interesting print ads. Don't limit yourself to magazines you already know. The wider your assortment, the more varied the ads you'll find. Next, select two ads and describe each one. Then analyze them by answering the questions below. If you wish, attach a photocopy of the ads.

- Does the advertisement motivate the viewers to think or merely appeal to their emotions? Explain.
- What hopes, fears, or desires, if any, is the ad designed to exploit? How does it appeal to them?
- What attitudes or values, if any, does the ad promote—for example, attitudes about success? How does it promote them?
- Do you share those attitudes and values?
- What propaganda techniques, if any, are used? Explain how they are used.
- Would you classify this ad as fair or unfair persuasion? What's the evidence for your view?

FIRST AD

Description:

_____

_____

Analysis:

_____

_____

_____

SECOND AD

Description:

_____

_____

Analysis:

_____

_____

_____

Thinking critically about television programming

By high school graduation the average person has spent 11,000 hours in the classroom and 22,000 hours watching television. All things being equal, television has twice as much impact on a person's mind as formal education.

Yet all things are not equal. Television producers have more means to maintain audience attention. They can use music to manipulate emotions. Directors can shift scenes to sustain interest and use applause tracks to cue responses. All this is evidence for television's impact. The question continues to be debated: Is that impact mainly positive or negative?

In 1961 Newton Minow, then chairman of the Federal Communications Commission, called television a "vast wasteland." Twenty-five years later his judgment was essentially the same. In Minow's view and those of other critics, television seriously underestimates the viewer's intelligence.

Other critics of television programming argue that it also creates mental habits and attitudes that hinder learning. These critics advance the following arguments:

- By keeping young people away from books, television denies them opportunities to develop imagination.
- Television aims programming at the lowest common denominator. This deprives young people of intellectual challenge.
- By feeding young people a steady diet of slang and clichés, television hinders their language skills.
- Television limits game show questions to who? what? where? and when?—seldom how? and never why? This creates the impression that knowledge of trivia is the only knowledge worth having. It also implies that careful analysis of issues is unnecessary or boring.
- Television uses the narrative approach for most of its programming. Examples are soap operas, sitcoms, movies, and dramatic

series. By doing so, television denies young people exposure to critical thinking. (Such thinking is more commonly expressed in analysis than in narrative.)

• Television fills the roster of talk shows with celebrities rather than authorities. By doing so, television creates the impression that it's not what you know but how well you are known that's important. It also promotes misinformation. For example, a television interviewer asked an actress, "Did your role in that television drama give you any insights into adoption fraud?" (That's about as sensible as asking an actor who played a surgeon how to perform an appendectomy, or asking an actor who played an auto mechanic how to overhaul an engine.) Not surprisingly, the actress did not hesitate to offer her opinion.

Jerry Mander has analyzed why television has failed to live up to expectations. In *Four Arguments for the Elimination of Television,* he claims that television has a number of inherent limitations that cannot easily be overcome. For one thing, it is an artificial environment that viewers have no hand in creating. Even on newscasts, we see only what others decide to show us, and always from their particular perspective and according to their priorities. For every item included in the news, thousands are excluded.

Another limitation is that less dramatic things don't play as well on television as more dramatic ones. That is why we see more angry expressions than happy ones, more fistfights and shootings than calm discussions, more car chases and explosions than tranquil scenes, more passionate sexual encounters than gentler expressions of friendship, caring, and tenderness.

A third limitation, according to Mander, is that the everyday pace of reality is not well suited to television. To make their stories interesting, programmers have to compress events. TV heroes are confronted by one dangerous situation after another, whereas in real life many tedious hours of inactivity intervene. Regular television viewing can create the unrealistic expectation that real life ought to be one peak experience after another.

The expectation is reinforced by the news. Reporters prefer to cover sensational stories. When they are forced to cover an ordinary event they often seek out the most dramatic or sensational aspect—for example, the single angry outburst in an otherwise calm and productive city council meeting. Antisocial behavior is deemed more newsworthy than social behavior.

The inherent limitations of television result in a number of biases in selecting program material. Mander finds more than thirty, including the following:

A bias for war over peace, and violence over nonviolence

A bias for superficiality over depth, simplification over balance

A bias for feelings of conflict over feelings of agreement

A bias for dissatisfaction over satisfaction, anger over tranquility, jealousy over acceptance

A bias for competition over cooperation

A bias for materialism over spirituality

A bias for the bizarre over the commonplace, the fixed over the evolutionary, the static over the dynamic

If these charges by Mander and others are valid, television may be responsible for a number of social problems. For example, it may cause or aggravate many of the difficulties students experience in school, some of which cause them to drop out before graduating. Television may also be responsible for the tendency of many people to settle for mediocrity rather than strive for excellence.

The following exercises direct your critical thinking to these questions: Is television programming harming our country and its citizens? If so, what can be done to correct that? If not, what can be done to make television programming an even more positive influence?

⬧ Exercise 66

Select a television game show and watch it for one or more programs. Note the way the game is played, the kinds of questions asked, and the time allowed for responses. Also note background effects such as music, lights, or revolving wheels and any other significant details about the show. Then analyze what you've seen. Answer these and any other relevant questions:

- How intellectually demanding is the show? What is its appeal to viewers?

_____

_____

- What habits or attitudes could this show develop or reinforce in regular adult viewers? In children? Will these habits and attitudes help or hinder life in school, on the job, and at home?

_____

_____

_____

Next, on a separate sheet of paper write a composition of at least several paragraphs expanding on your findings.

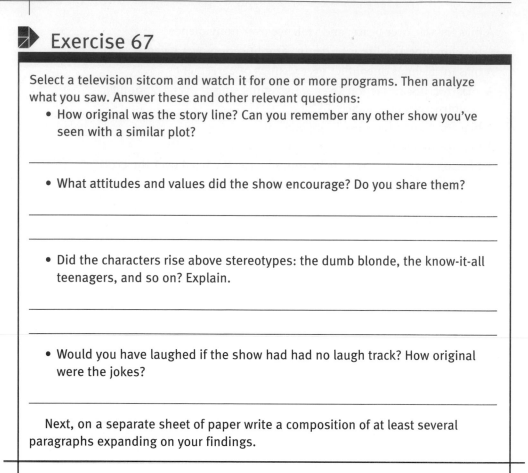

Exercise 67

Select a television sitcom and watch it for one or more programs. Then analyze what you saw. Answer these and other relevant questions:

- How original was the story line? Can you remember any other show you've seen with a similar plot?

_____

- What attitudes and values did the show encourage? Do you share them?

_____

_____

- Did the characters rise above stereotypes: the dumb blonde, the know-it-all teenagers, and so on? Explain.

_____

_____

- Would you have laughed if the show had had no laugh track? How original were the jokes?

_____

   Next, on a separate sheet of paper write a composition of at least several paragraphs expanding on your findings.

Exercise 68

Choose a television drama—a soap opera, detective or western show, or a movie. To help yourself think critically, pick a show you don't normally see. Watch the show and then analyze what you saw. Answer these and any other relevant questions:

- Which characters did the show present favorably? What was the main action taken by each of those characters during the show?

_____

_____

- Think about the characters you chose in the above question. What view would each express on the following topics?

Exercise 68 (cont.)

Reasoning with others:

Violence:

Sexual relationships:

Marriage:

Authority:

Success:

- Did the show include any incidents of violence and/or destruction? If so, describe them and explain whether their depiction was essential to the plot.

- Were people or principles betrayed during the show? If so, describe each incident and explain whether the betrayal was presented in a positive or a negative light.

- Did the show emphasize antagonism or harmony? Were issues resolved peacefully or violently? Explain.

On a separate sheet of paper write a composition of at least several paragraphs explaining whether the show you watched promoted desirable attitudes and habits.

▶ Exercise 69

Skim the television talk-show listings. Then select a show and watch it. Analyze what you saw, answering these and any other relevant questions:

- What was the show's theme or discussion topic?

_____

- What fields did the guests represent: show business, education, particular professions, or others? Are the guests associated with specific attitudes, values, behaviors? If so, describe those attitudes, values, or behaviors.

_____

_____

- What was the reason why each appeared on the show? For example, an author may have published a new book or an actress may have starred in a just-released film.

_____

_____

- What kinds of questions did the host ask? Professional questions? Personal questions? Questions that seemed outside the person's expertise?

_____

_____

- Were any specific attitudes and values encouraged? If so, what were they?

_____

_____

- How much time did the host allow for each answer? Did the guest have an opportunity to elaborate on answers? How much time was devoted to each guest?

_____

_____

- How many times was the discussion interrupted by commercial breaks?

_____

_____

Next, write a composition of at least several paragraphs on a separate sheet of paper. Focus on this question: Would regular viewing of talk shows like the one you watched be good preparation for the probing discussions conducted in college classrooms?

⮞ Exercise 70

Watch the evening newscast on FOX News Channel (this is not the same as the Fox channel that shows situation comedies and movies). Then watch the newscast on one of the following: CNN, CBS, NBC, ABC. Compare their presentations of the news. Answer these and any other relevant questions:

- How much time, on average, was given to each news story?

_____

_____

- What details did the newscasters focus on? What questions did they pass over? Did you want answers to any of the latter questions?

_____

_____

- How were the newscasts similar? Look, for example, at the numbers and genders of the newscasters, construction of the studio sets, and each show's format. How were the shows different?

_____

_____

- How many commercial breaks occurred during the newscast?

_____

_____

- Did the news reports offer different perspectives on the events reported on?

_____

_____

- What other types of stories might have been included?

_____

_____

On a separate sheet of paper write a composition explaining which network you would recommend to someone looking for a fair and objective presentation of the news. Be sure you offers reasons for your choice.

> **Exercise 71**

Consider the observations and judgments of the various kinds of television programming from the previous exercises. Decide what changes would improve television programming. Then, on a separate sheet of paper, write a letter to the Federal Communications Commission. State your ideas for improving programming and give reasons for acting on those ideas.

Thinking critically about movies

Some people believe critical thinking has little application to movies because movies are an art form—representations of life designed to give pleasure rather than arguments offered to persuade people.

This view is an example of either/or thinking. It assumes that entertainment and persuasion are mutually exclusive. They are not. Moviemakers often want both to create a work of art *and* to influence people's thinking. In some cases, the persuasive intention takes precedence.

It is true that movies almost never present ideas directly in the manner of non-fiction writing. Nevertheless, ideas are embedded in the stories. Simply said, they show the ideas rather than tell them. The effect is more emotional than intellectual, but no less potent for that.

If a filmmaker wants to hold an idea up to ridicule, for example, he need only create a character who holds that idea and make him or her appear ridiculous.

In order to think critically about movies, you must understand the various elements. The basic ones are the same as those in short stories, novels, and plays.

Characters

Every story has one or more main characters, and often a number of secondary ones. The way the characters are presented will influence the audience's reaction to them.

Setting

The elements of setting are time, place, and the circumstances in which the story takes place.

Plot

The plot is the sequence of events that occurs in the story. The essential element in a movie plot is *conflict*. A challenge or problem confronts the characters and they struggle to solve it. The conflict may be external or merely within the character's mind.

Theme

The theme of a movie is the message or lesson it offers. The theme is almost never stated directly, though the dialog may contain statements that clearly imply it.

In addition to the basic elements, movies have three other elements not found in written literature—the performances of the actors, sound effects, and visual effects. Sound effects include background music as well as dialogue. Visual effects are created by moving the camera in for close-up shots or out for distance shots, as well as by varying the lighting and camera angles.

In thinking critically about movies, it is important to evaluate each of the elements and make a balanced judgment. Seldom will a movie be uniformly excellent in all elements. The characters, for example, may be richly drawn and the plot plausible and ingenious. Yet the acting may be poor and the theme an insult to the viewer's intelligence.

The Golden Globe and Academy Awards reflect these distinctions. Rarely will a film "sweep" the awards. And even when it succeeds in doing so, or comes close, critical thinking will sometimes reveal serious weaknesses.

Consider, for example, the film that won a host of Academy Awards in the year 2000, *American Beauty*. (The awards included Best Picture, Best Actor, Best Screenplay, and Best Cinematography.)

The film is the story of Lester Burnam (played by Kevin Spacey) in the throes of a mid-life crisis. He quits his job, becomes obsessed with and nearly seduces his daughter's teenage girlfriend, and begins smoking marijuana purchased from his daughter's boyfriend. Only after he dies does he gain the (unoriginal) "insight" that our lives are quite small and insignificant compared to the vastness of the cosmos.

In the opinion of some reviewers all four adults are seriously disturbed. Lester's neighbor is a homophobic Marine with secret homosexual urges. The neighbor's browbeaten wife is nearly catatonic. Lester's wife puts work above family and cheats on her husband with a fellow real estate agent, who is shallow and self-absorbed.

In contrast, all the teenagers are both pure of heart and wise. In fact, the drug pusher boyfriend has the controlling insight of the film, which Lester has to die to realize.

To sum up, *American Beauty* portrays adults as contemptible if not corrupt, especially those who represent discipline, order, and responsibility. Teenagers, on the other hand, are wonderful. Among the questions critical thinking raises about this film are these: Are the characterizations of adults and teenagers plausible? How reasonable is the theme?

Exercise 72

Visit the Rotten Tomatoes website at www.rottentomatoes.com or another site that reviews current movies. Then follow the directions for EITHER "A" or "B" below:

A

Access the complete list of current box office film titles. Scan the list of films and find one that you have seen. Click on that title and access the excerpts from reviews. Find two that agree with your assessment of the film and two that disagree. Then click on each of the review excerpts, access the full review, and read it. On a separate sheet of paper, write a brief paper answering these questions: Did the reviews help you deepen your insight into the meaning and/or quality of the film? What are your strongest points of agreement and disagreement with the reviewers?

B

Click on the various film titles and read the plot synopses. (Note: The synopses are available in both brief and full format.) Then, on a separate sheet of paper, write a brief composition that answers this question: Do you find more similarities or dissimilarities of plot and theme? Explain your answer with specific references to the films.

Exercise 73

Select a movie you have recently seen; or, if you wish, rent a video and watch it. Then evaluate the film on a separate sheet of paper. Follow this format:
1. State the name of the film.
2. Identify the main and important secondary characters and the setting.
3. Explain the plot and identify what you believe to be the theme.
4. Judge the film's strengths and weaknesses.

Thinking critically about music

Ridiculing another generation's music has long been a popular pastime. Someone once defined an opera as an art form in which anything that is too dumb to be spoken is sung. Another person observed that classical music threatens to develop a tune with every other bar and then disappoints us. A third termed jazz an appeal to the emotions by an attack on the nerves. Another, writing of rock music, suggested that the proper pitch for most electric guitars is right out the window, followed by the player.

Yet the fact that each generation prefers its own music does not mean that all criticism is without merit. It is important to keep this in mind in evaluating contemporary music.

Music has changed greatly in the past half-century, perhaps more so than in any comparable period in history. In the late 1940s two older musical traditions continued in vogue. One was Big Band music, played for ballroom dancing ranging from the elegant foxtrot to frenetic jitterbugging. The other was jazz.

The 1950s brought rock and roll with its very different beat, both literally and figuratively. It may have lacked the refinement and style of jazz, but there was no doubting its raucous energy. From the days of Elvis Presley's "Blue Suede Shoes" to the present, rock and roll has undergone several transformations, notably to acid rock and then heavy metal. And other music forms have become popular—reggae, for example, and rap.

The differences between 1940s music and today's music go beyond the overall sound or the beat. Because no amplification existed then, the loudest jazz band was much quieter than today's groups. In those days, too, singers still crooned ballads in the manner of Bing Crosby and Frank Sinatra. Lyrics were meant to be understood and the singer's voice was regarded as another fine instrument to be used with precision to produce pleasant, melodious sounds. Singers wore hair styles no different from those of business people. All that has changed.

A more significant difference than these is the ideas and attitudes conveyed by the lyrics themselves and the mannerisms that accompany them. Today's lyrics and stage antics would have been unimaginable fifty years ago. Many popular videos celebrate the destruction of property, rape, child abuse, incest, sadism, murder, and suicide. Onscreen images depict these behaviors in graphic detail. And the average age of the audience that watches them is between 14 and 16.

Critics of contemporary music have charged that it is undermining the fundamental values of society and causing antisocial attitudes and behavior, including crime. Spokespeople for the music industry tend to dismiss such criticism, claiming that musicians are only exercising their right of free expression and no one can be harmed by that. The exercises that follow will give you an opportunity to examine this issue.

Exercise 74

Visit a music store and examine a number of current CDs or cassettes. Note the cover designs, song titles, and lyrics. Listen to releases from major groups. Then, on a separate sheet of paper, list each CD or cassette you examined and record your observations.

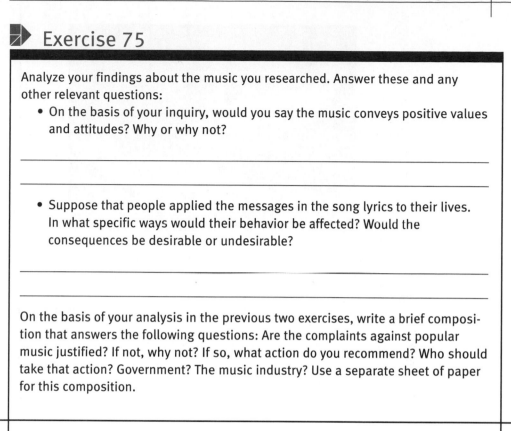

Thinking critically about magazines

Literally hundreds of magazines are available on a variety of subjects, including animals, art, investment, computers, entertainment, hobbies, home and garden, nature, religion, science, and travel. Among the most widely read are news magazines such as *Time, Newsweek,* and *U.S. News and World Report.* Also popular are the general interest tabloid magazines such as *People, The Star,* and *The National Enquirer.*

Some magazines publish only staff-written articles. Others solicit articles from freelance writers. Every magazine has its own specific areas of interest, format, editorial requirements, and point of view.

A magazine's target audience may be broad, as in the case of most news magazines, or narrow. There are magazines for political conservatives and magazines for liberals, some for men and others for women. Age, marital status, and work status are further areas of specialization.

McCall's, for example, is published for women in general; *Redbook,* for young mothers, ages 25–44; *Cosmopolitan,* for working women, 18–35, who are single, married, or divorced.

Among the most common criticisms of news and/or general interest magazines are the following:

- The editorial biases of news magazines often result in a lack of objectivity in reporting, particularly on issues related to bias. A secular bias, for example, might prejudice the treatment of religion; a liberal political bias might prejudice the treatment of conservative proposals or programs.
- General interest magazines often promote shallowness and superficiality by focusing on the details of celebrities' lives, particularly scandalous details.
- Many magazines allow their choice and treatment of subject matter to be influenced—and often compromised—by their advertisers.
- Many magazines tend to reinforce the values of popular culture—in particular, impulsiveness, self-indulgence, and instant gratification—rather than the values of traditional culture.

The following exercises invite you to apply critical thinking and decide whether these charges are valid. To complete these assignments you may decide to visit a newsstand, a library, or a bookstore.

⏩ Exercise 76

Examine the current editions of several news magazines—*Time, Newsweek,* and *U.S. News and World Report*—or one written from a particular ethnic perspective. Select a single news item and compare the treatment it is given in each magazine. Decide which magazine's treatment is most biased and which is least biased. Support your findings.

   Your decision and explanation:

_____

_____

_____

_____

_____

_____

_____

_____

⏩ Exercise 77

Check the covers of the current issues of magazines such as *Cosmopolitan, McCall's, Esquire, Redbook,* and *Psychology Today.* (Feel free to include any other magazine to which you subscribe or in which you are interested.) Compare the titles of the articles listed on the covers. Do these titles raise any questions about the magazines' themes, focuses, or editorial perspectives? Explain your findings.

_____

_____

_____

_____

_____

_____

_____

_____

_____

Exercise 78

Examine an edition of each of the following publications: *The Star, The National Enquirer,* and *People.* Read the articles, the special sections, and the advice columns. Sample the ads and look closely at the photographs. Then answer these questions:

- Suppose that a stranger to this country were to draw a conclusion about our society's attitudes and values just from reading these publications. What conclusion do you think she would draw? What about these periodicals leads you to this conclusion?

_____

_____

_____

_____

_____

- Do you think these publications merely reflect our society's attitudes and values or do they also help shape those attitudes and values? Explain.

_____

_____

_____

_____

On a separate sheet of paper, write a brief composition explaining what changes in format and emphasis would you recommend to improve these publications?

Thinking critically about newspapers

The newspaper is an ancient form of communication that can be traced back to about 59 B.C.E. when the Roman *Acta Diurna* was posted in public places. Its greatest development, however, occurred after

the invention of printing in the fifteenth century. More recently, the invention of the telegraph, the photocomposition process, and the communications satellite have made news gathering and publication faster and more efficient.

Other inventions, however, have challenged the newspaper's position as the leading provider of information. The most notable of these inventions have been radio and television, and the personal computer has similar potential. All three make news available at the flip of a switch, whereas the newspaper is available, in most cases, only once a day.

The newspaper has a further disadvantage—it requires the effort of reading. In contrast, broadcast news is obtained effortlessly, and in a conveniently rapid pace, in moving pictures. In reaction to this handicap, the newspaper industry has simplified and shortened stories. A good example of this approach is the *USA Today* format.

Another change in print journalism over the past few decades concerns the treatment of fact and opinion. Traditionally, news stories presented only facts, objectively and without comment. A special place was reserved for commentary—the op-ed page (the term is short for opinion-editorial). There the reader would find editorials presenting the newspaper's official point of view on issues of the day, letters expressing readers' reactions to previous news stories, and opinion essays written by professional columnists.

Today's newspapers still have op-ed pages, with editorials, letters, and columns. But opinion is not always carefully screened out of news stories. Many journalists blend their interpretations and personal judgments into the news. Only the alert reader will understand where reporting ends and editorializing begins.

The op-ed page is often the most rewarding part of the newspaper because it is filled with lively analysis of current issues. The following exercises invite you to apply your critical thinking skills to that page.

▨ Exercise 79

Choose the largest newspaper in your area or a newspaper serving a larger audience, such as *USA Today*. Read the main editorial of the day. Also read any news story mentioned in the editorial. Then, on a separate sheet of paper, answer the following questions:

- What position does the editor take on the issue? What support does he or she offer for this position?
- What other positions could be taken on the issue? How might those positions be supported? Before answering these questions, you may wish to research the issue by visiting the library or interviewing experts.
- What are the editorial's strengths and weaknesses?
- What position is most reasonable in light of the evidence? Present your response in a composition of at least several paragraphs. Another option is to write your response as a letter to the editor. If you do this, consider sending the letter to the newspaper.

▨ Exercise 80

Select an opinion column or a letter to the editor that interests you. Examine it critically. If appropriate, research the issue further. Then, on a separate sheet of paper, write a composition of at least several paragraphs stating and supporting your position on the issue. You may agree with the article or letter in the newspaper, disagree with it, or agree in part. Attach either a summary or a copy of the original article or letter.

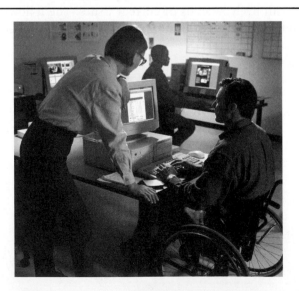

Thinking critically about the Internet

"LET THE BROWSER BEWARE!"

"SURF AT YOUR OWN RISK"

Don't expect to find these warnings on the Internet. The ideas you find there have not been screened by a board of standards for accuracy or reasonableness. No logic police force patrols the Internet looking for violators. It is up to you to avoid being victimized. The critical thinking strategy you have been using throughout this book is your best protection. Here are the most important questions to ask whenever you use the Internet:

Whose site is this?

You will likely visit many different sites, including government (.gov), education (.edu), and commercial (.com) sites. Each site will most likely reflect the bias and/or agenda of the people who created and maintain it. Knowing whose site it is will help you evaluate the reliability of the information you find there.

What function does the site serve?

Every site has a specific purpose. Generally speaking, government and education sites are designed to provide the public with important or helpful information. In contrast, commercial sites are designed to sell products and/or services.

Expect the companies that have commercial websites to say good things about their own products and services and to ignore shortcomings and flaws. Don't be surprised if they imply that their competitors' products and services are inferior. Be aware that such statements and implications may or may not be true and should be tested rather than taken at face value.

As was pointed out in "Conducting Internet Research" in Chapter Four, you can eliminate commercial websites from your Google searches by adding at the end of your search term the minus sign followed (without a space) by ".com." For example, if you were searching for vitamin therapy you would type *vitamin therapy-.com.*

Which statements are fact and which are opinion?

A fact is a generally accepted reality, a matter that informed people agree about. An opinion, on the other hand, is a belief or a conclusion open to dispute. Once we accept something as a fact, we are no longer inclined to think critically about it. That is why it is important not to confuse opinion with fact.

Such confusion is potentially greater on the Internet than in print or broadcast media because the dissemination of ideas is easier on the Internet. Anyone can say anything on the Internet and reach a worldwide audience. Not surprisingly, rumormongers, manipulators, and other mischief makers have flocked there.

To keep your critical thinking sharp, regard all statements as opinions unless you are certain they are universally endorsed.

Where can statements of fact be confirmed?

Statements that are offered as factual may in reality be false. (Even honest people make mistakes, and not everyone is honest.) Suppose you encounter the statement "The divorce rate has tripled in the past twenty years." This is clearly a *statement* of fact. But is it factual? In other words, is it accurate? Prudence suggests that you seek confirmation by looking in an almanac or other statistical record.

The nature of the statement will determine where you can find verification. To confirm the statement that a congressional candidate was once convicted of sexual harassment, for example, you would check appropriate court records or, at the very least, determine what other sources, if any, support the claim. Endorsement of the statement by the candidate's opponents would mean little; admission by his or her political *allies* would be significant.

How widely shared is this opinion?
What do authorities on the subject think of it?

Knowing whether an opinion is shared by a majority or a minority will not tell you how reasonable it is. Minority opinions are not necessarily inferior. Many great insights can be traced to a single individual's advancing an unpopular view. But for every minority view that eventually is proven right, several are proven wrong.

To put it simply, the odds favor the consensus views of informed people. Identify the full range of opinions on the issue by consulting other Internet websites that deal with the topic in question. (Also, consult print and broadcast media sources.) Hesitate to accept any opinion that is rejected by most informed people, as well as any opinion about which informed people are sharply divided.

Is the reasoning behind the opinion logical?

Look specifically for the following errors, which were discussed in Chapter Five, "Recognizing Errors in Thinking." Each of them can be found in many places, including websites:

Errors of perception: "mine is better" thinking, selective perception, gullibility and skepticism, bias toward the majority or the minority, pretending to know, bias for or against change, either/or thinking.

Errors of judgment: double standard, irrelevant criterion, overgeneralizing or stereotyping, hasty conclusion, unwarranted assumption, failure to make a distinction, oversimplification.

Errors of reaction: explaining away, shifting the burden of proof, attacking the person, straw man.

Does the evidence support the opinion?

In making this decision, consider all the evidence you have found. That includes the evidence offered in support of the opinion and the evidence you found in searching the Internet and other information sources. Remember, too, that your own personal observation and experience, if relevant to the issue, count as evidence.

⏩ Exercise 81

We tend to take airline safety for granted. But when a serious accident or terrorist attack occurs anywhere in the world, the public begins questioning how safe air travel is in this country. The issue has many facets, including the age and condition of aircraft, the quality of maintenance, and the adequacy of air traffic control procedures and equipment. Investigate this issue on the Internet, using Google and the resource list you developed in Chapter Four. Then, on a separate sheet of paper, report the sites you consulted and what you found there. Finally, apply the critical thinking strategy you have been using throughout this book. State your conclusion and the reasoning that led you to it.

⏩ Exercise 82

The issue of term limits concerns whether elected officials at the local, state, and/or national levels should be allowed to remain in office indefinitely or be limited to, say, two or three consecutive terms. Investigate this issue on the Internet, being careful to consider both pro and con arguments. Next, on a separate sheet of paper, report the sites you consulted and what you found there. Finally, apply the critical thinking strategy explained in this chapter to evaluate your findings. State your conclusion and the reasoning that led you to it.

▰▶ Exercise 83

Although sex education has been a part of most elementary and secondary curriculums for many years, it remains controversial. There has been sharp division on a number of matters including these:

Is sex education helping to solve the problem of teen pregnancy or aggravating it?

Do the methods and materials used in sex education support or challenge community standards?

Should parents be given a larger role in the development of sex education programs?

Investigate these and related questions on the Internet, being careful to consider both pro and con arguments. Next, on a separate sheet of paper, report the sites you consulted and what you found there. Finally, apply the critical thinking strategy explained in this chapter to evaluate your findings. State your conclusion and the reasoning that led you to it.

▰▶ Exercise 84

Imagine that you've decided to buy a new car and need to find the best terms on an auto loan. Search the Internet, identify a number of lenders, and compare the terms they offer. Summarize your findings on a separate sheet of paper. Then decide which lender would be the best one for you and explain your reasoning in a brief composition.

☑ quiz

Write your answer on a separate sheet of paper.

1. List the four steps used in solving a problem.

2. How many guidelines are offered for successful relationships? Briefly explain the one you find most helpful to you personally.

3. In choosing a career, only one factor is important—what you would *like* to do. True or false? Explain.

4. State and briefly explain each of the three criteria for making ethical judgments.

☑ quiz (cont.)

5. Newton Minow believes that television has improved significantly over the past quarter-century. True or false? Explain.

6. Explain two common criticisms of magazine publishing.

7. The first newspaper was published in the nineteenth century. True or false? Explain.

8. Identify two criticisms commonly made of popular music.

9. Define each of the following terms:
   Bandwagon

   Glittering generality

   Empty comparison

   Meaningless slogan

   Testimonial

   Transfer

   Stacking the deck

   Misleading statement

10. Explain two criticisms commonly made of print advertising.

11. The function of most commercial websites is to provide a public service. True or false? Explain.

12. Name the elements to examine when evaluating a movie.

KRAUPNER PHARMACY

"N.Y.'S LARGEST DRUG INVENTORY"

Broadhead . com

---

457 Knickerbocker Ave • Brooklyn, NY 11237
Ph. 718-821-1313 • Fax. 718-821-2665

Epilogue

Make the end a beginning

You've finished reading this book and completed its exercises and other opportunities to practice critical thinking. Now you have a choice. You can decide that this moment will mark the end of one more academic experience. If this is your choice, just consign the book to a box in your basement and let it gather dust. As memory fades, the experiences you had with this book will be lost.

On the other hand, you can decide to make this book and critical thinking skills a vital part of your life. You can choose to make the end a beginning. One strategy is to buy a notebook and continue the journal you began here. If you use an actual notebook, as opposed to a computer document, use the left pages for recording observations and reserve the right pages for reflecting on those observations. Since your reflections are likely to be lengthier than your observations, leave appropriate space between observations.

Here is a collection of quotations to help you get started. Some apply in many situations, others in a limited number. A few may need qualification. All will provide excellent food for thought. *Bon appétit!*

If I am not for myself, who will be? If I am only for myself, what am I?
    —Rabbi Hillel

Someone's boring me . . . I think it's me. —Dylan Thomas

A great many people think they are thinking when they are merely rearranging their prejudices. —William James

Each morning puts a man on trial and each evening passes judgment. —Roy L. Smith

There are two ways of exerting one's strength: one is pushing down, and the other is pulling up. —Booker T. Washington

Happiness is not a state to arrive at, but a manner of traveling. —Margaret Lee Rumbeck

How glorious it is—and how painful—to be an exception. —Alfred de Musset

The man who most vividly realizes a difficulty is the man most likely to overcome it. —Joseph Farrell

You can tell the ideals of a nation by its advertisements. —Norman Douglas

That man is the richest whose pleasures are the cheapest. —Henry David Thoreau

To read without reflecting is like eating without digesting. —Edmund Burke

Remember, no one can make you feel inferior without your consent. —Eleanor Roosevelt

Trend is not destiny. —Lewis Mumford

Success is a journey, not a destination. —Ben Sweetland

Many people's tombstones should read "Died at 30. Buried at 60." —Nicholas Murray Butler

Victory has a hundred fathers, but defeat is an orphan. —Count G. Ciano

A cathedral, a wave of a storm, a dancer's leap, never turn out to be as high as we had hoped. —Marcel Proust

Men are not punished for their sins, but by them. —Elbert G. Hubbard

Never has a man who has bent himself been able to make others straight. —Mencius

Free will does not mean one will, but many wills in one [person]. —Flannery O'Connor

The offender never forgives. —Russian proverb

No matter which side of an argument you're on, you always find some people on your side that you wish were on the other side. —Jascha Heifetz

Works Cited

Adler, Mortimer J. *The Great Ideas: A Lexicon of Western Thought*. New York: Macmillan, 1992.

Albom, Mitch. *The Five People You Meet in Heaven*. New York: Hyperion, 2003.

Bruce, Tammy. *The New Thought Police*. New York: Prima Publishing, 2001.

Carnegie, Dale. *How to Win Friends and Influence People*. New York: Pocket Books, 1990.

Cerf, Christopher, and Victor Navasky. *The Experts Speak*. New York: Villard, 1984, 1998.

Curtsinger, Bill. "Close Encounters with the Gray Reef Shark," *National Geographic*, January, 1995, 45–67.

Frankl, Viktor. *Man's Search for Meaning*, 3rd edition. New York: Simon & Schuster, 1984.

Goldberg, Bernard. *Bias*. Washington, DC, Regnery Publishing, 2002.

——— *Arrogance*. New York: Warner Books, 2003.

Harris, Errol E. "Respect for Persons," *Dædalus*, Spring 1969.

Hoe, Philip Chew Kheng, editor. *A Gentleman's Code: According to Confucius, Mencius and Others*. Singapore: Graham Brash (Pte) Ltd, 1984.

Kohn, Alfie. "The Truth About Self-Esteem," *Phi Delta Kappan*, December 1994, 272–283.

L'Amour, Louis. *Education of a Wandering Man*. New York: Bantam Books, 1989.

Loftus, Elizabeth. *Witness for the Defense*. New York: St. Martin's Press, 1991.

———. *Eyewitness Testimony*. Cambridge, MA: Harvard University Press, 1996.

Mander, Jerry. *Four Arguments for the Elimination of Television*. New York: Quill, 1978.

McGowan, William. *Coloring the News*. San Francisco: Encounter Books, 2001.

Pisar, Samuel. *Of Blood and Hope*. New York: Little, Brown, 1980.

Rogers, Carl. *On Becoming a Person*. Boston: Houghton Mifflin, 1961.

Samenow, Stanton. *Inside the Criminal Mind.* New York: Times Books, 1984.

Schlesinger, Arthur, Jr. *The Disuniting of America: Reflections on a Multi-cultural Society.* New York: W.W. Norton, 1992.

Sowell, Thomas. *Race and Culture.* New York: Basic Books, 1994.

Stevenson, Harold, and James Stigler. *The Learning Gap.* New York: Simon & Schuster, 1992.

Tavris, Carol. *Anger: The Misunderstood Emotion.* New York: Simon & Schuster, 1982.

————. *The Mismeasure of Woman.* New York: Simon & Schuster, 1992.

Underhill, Jack. "New Age Quiz," *Life Times*, no.3, 6.

Vitz, Paul. *Faith of the Fatherless.* Dallas: Spence Publishing Co., 1999.

Bibliography

The following books on critical thinking and related subjects can help you deepen your understanding and expand your skill.

Adams, James. *Conceptual Blockbusting.* New York: W. W. Norton, 1979.

Adler, Mortimer. *Intellect: Mind Over Matter.* New York: Macmillan Publishing Co., 1990.

————. *How to Read a Book.* New York: Simon & Schuster, 1972.

Barker, Evelyn M. *Everyday Reasoning.* Englewood Cliffs, NJ: Prentice-Hall, 1981.

Barry, Vincent E., and Joel Rudinow. *Invitation to Critical Thinking.* New York: Harcourt Brace, 1998.

Browne, M. Neil, and Stuart M. Keely. *Asking the Right Questions: A Guide to Critical Thinking,* 7th ed. Englewood Cliffs, NJ: Prentice-Hall, 2004.

Cederblom, J. B., and David W. Paulsen. *Critical Reasoning,* 5th ed. Belmont, CA: Wadsworth Publishing Co., 2001.

Chaffee, John. *Thinking Critically,* 8th ed. New York: Houghton Mifflin, 2006.

Damer, Edward. *Attacking Faulty Reasoning,* 5th ed. Belmont, CA: Wadsworth Publishing Co., 2005.

DeBono, Edward. *Lateral Thinking.* New York: Harper & Row, 1970.

Engel, Morris S. *With Good Reason: An Introduction to Informal Fallacies,* 6th ed. New York: St. Martin's Press, 2000.

Fischer, David Hackett. *Historians' Fallacies: Toward a Logic of Historical Thought.* New York: Harper Perennial, 1970.

Fisher, Alec. *The Logic of Real Arguments.* New York: Cambridge University Press, 2001.

Gilovich, Thomas. *How We Know What Isn't So: The Fallibility of Reason in Everyday Life.* New York: Free Press, 1991.

Goldberg, Bernard. *Bias.* Washington, DC: Regnery Publishing, 2002.

Gould, Stephen Jay. *The Mismeasure of Man.* New York: W. W. Norton, 1981.

Govier, Trudy. *A Practical Study of Argument,* 5th ed. Belmont, CA: Wadsworth Publishing Co., 2001.

Halpern, Diane. *Thought and Knowledge.* Hillsdale, NJ: Lawrence Erlbaum, 2002.

Hoaglund, John. *Critical Thinking.* Newport News, VA: Vale Press, 1995.

Hofstadter, Richard. *Anti-Intellectualism in American Life.* New York: Vintage, 1963.

Johnson, Ralph, and J. A. Blair. *Logical Self-Defense.* New York: McGraw-Hill, 1994.

Kohn, Bob. *Journalistic Fraud: How The New York Times Distorts the News and Why It Can No Longer Be Trusted.* Nashville, TN: WND Books, 2003.

Kytle, Ray. *Clear Thinking for Composition,* 5th ed. New York: McGraw-Hill, 1988.

Langer, Ellen J. *Mindfulness.* Reading, MA: Addison-Wesley, 1989.

Lazere, Donald. *American Media and Mass Culture.* Berkeley, CA: University of California Press, 1987.

Mander, Jerry. *Four Arguments for the Elimination of Television.* New York: Quill Publishing, 1978.

Mayfield, Marlys. *Thinking for Yourself: Developing Critical Thinking Skills Through Reading and Writing,* 5th ed. Boston: Heinle & Heinle, 2003.

Moore, Noel, and Richard Parker. *Critical Thinking.* New York: McGraw-Hill, 2003.

Moore, W. Edgar and others. *Creative and Critical Thinking.* Boston: Houghton Mifflin, 1984.

Nickerson, Raymond S. *Reflections on Reasoning.* Hillsdale, NJ: Lawrence Erlbaum, 1986.

Nisbett, Richard, and Lee Ross. *Human Inference: Strategies and Short-comings of Social Judgment.* Englewood Cliffs, NJ: Prentice-Hall, 1980.

Paul, Richard, and Linda Elder. *Critical Thinking.* Englewood Cliffs, NJ: Prentice-Hall, 2001.

Perkins, David. *Archimedes Bathtub: The Art and Logic of Breakthrough Thinking.* New York: W. W. Norton, 2000.

Postman, Neil. *Amusing Ourselves to Death.* New York: Oxford University Press, 1985.

Rosenthal, Peggy. *Words and Values.* New York: Oxford University Press, 1984.

Ruggiero, Vincent Ryan. *The Art of Thinking,* 4th ed. New York: HarperCollins, 2004.

——. *Beyond Feelings: A Guide to Critical Thinking.* Mountain View, CA: Mayfield Publishing Co., 2004.

————. *Thinking Critically About Ethical Issues.* Mountain View, CA: Mayfield Publishing Co., 2004.

————. *Warning: Nonsense Is Destroying America.* Nashville, TN: Thomas Nelson, 1994.

Scriven, Michael. *Reasoning.* New York: McGraw-Hill, 1997.

Seech, Zachary. *Open Minds and Everyday Reasoning,* 2nd ed. Belmont, CA: Wadsworth Publishing Co., 2005.

Siegel, Harvey. *Relativism Refuted.* Norwell, MA: Kluwer Academic Publishers, 1987.

Sutherland, Stuart. *Irrationality: Why We Don't Think Straight!* New Brunswick, NJ: Rutgers University Press, 1994.

Thornton, Bruce S. *Plagues of the Mind: The New Epidemic of False Knowledge.* Wilmington, DE: ISI Books, 1999.

Toulmin, Stephen. *The Uses of Argument.* New York: Cambridge University Press, 2003.

Toulmin, Stephen E., Richard Rieke, and Alan Janik. *An Introduction to Reasoning.* Englewood Cliffs, NJ: Prentice-Hall, 1997.

Von Oech, Roger. *A Whack on the Side of the Head.* New York: HarperCollins, 1993.

————. *A Kick in the Seat of the Pants.* New York: Harper & Row, 1986.

Weaver, Richard, *Ideas Have Consequences.* Chicago: University of Chicago Press, 1948.

Weddle, Perry. *Argument.* New York: McGraw-Hill, 1978.

Index

Advertising
  print, 172–173
  techniques of, 168–170
Albom, Mitch, 155
"And" relationships, 102
Anecdotes and cases-in-point, 97
Arguments
  explanation of, 88
  Internet research and, 91–93
  interviewing and, 94, 95
  library research and, 89–90, 91
  original strategy vs revised strategy, 89
  strategy to evaluate complex, 101–106, 107
  against television programming, 175, 176
Assumptions, 126–127, 128
Attacking the person, 135
Attitudes
  culture and, 62
  definition and explanation of, 61
  evaluating, 62
  types of empowering, 66–68
Audience, 35

Bandwagon, 168
Bias
  change and, 121
  critical thinking and, 107–109
  of magazines, 188
  majority or minority, 121
  reporting, 69, 70
  in television programming, 176–177
Blair, Eric, 41
Bly, Nellie, 77
Bruce, Tammy, 70, 71, 72

Burden of proof, 134, 135
"But" relationships, 102

Careers
  approach to choosing, 158, 159
  errors in choosing, 156–157, 158
Carnegie, Dale, 36
Cerf, Bennett, 9
Characters, 183
Cochrane, Elizabeth, 77
Commercials
  advertising and, 167–170
  appeals of, 168
  print advertising in, 172–173
Communication
  newspapers and, 190–191
  persuasion, 32–51
Comparison, empty, 168
Complexity, 82
Conclusions, 126
Confucius, 68
Confusion, 80
Connectivity, 82
Contradiction, 7–8
Criteria, 124
Critical thinking
  bias and, 107–109
  careers and, 156–158, 159
  commercials and, 167–170
  ethical judgment and, 159–165
  evaluating attitudes and, 62
  ideas and, 11
  instruction in, 4, 5
  Internet and, 193–194, 195
  magazines and, 187–188
  movies and, 182–184
  music and, 185–186
  newspapers and, 190–191
  print advertising, 172–173
  relationships and, 150–155

television programming and, 175–177
  testing opinions and, 16–19
Criticism, 67, 124
Culture, 62

Dalton, Skye, 147
Dewey, Melvil, 90
Discovered truth, 5–6
Dishonesty, 70, 71, 173.
  See also Plagiarism
Dissent, suppressed, 71, 72
Distinctions, 128, 129
Double standard, 123, 124
Dyer, Wayne, 17

Edison, Thomas, 68
Effort, 67, 68
Ego. See Errors
Either/or thinking, 122, 182
Ellis, Albert, 5
Emotional, language, 70, 71
Empty comparison, 168
Epictetus, 16
Errors
  of judgment, 123–133, 194
  kinds of, 118–136
  multiplying of, 138
  of perception, 118–122, 194
  of reaction, 134–136, 194
Errors, overcoming
  in grammar, 42–44, 45
  in usage, 45–45, 47
Erskine, George, 16
Ethical judgments
  applying criteria for, 164
  criteria for making, 162–163
  definition of, 159
  explanation of, 161, 162
Evidence
  evaluating, 21–22, 105–106, 107

Internet and, 195
types of, 97–100, 101
Expectations, 37
Experiments, 100
Expert testimony, 98
Explaining away, 134
Eyewitness testimony, 98

Faber, Frederick W., 153
Facts
checking, 15, 16
complex arguments and,
101–104
Internet and, 193, 194
opinions *vs,* 12–14
persuasion and, 36
print journalism and, 191
Feeling *vs* thinking, 11, 12
First impressions, 79
Frankl, Viktor, 59
Freud, Sigmund, 97

Gates, Bill, 39
Generalizations, 124–125
Glittering generality, 168
Goldberg, Bernard, 69
Good Thinking!
Aaron Feuerstein, 152
Albert Einstein, 3
Carol Tavris, 125
Chiara Lubich, 163
Dale Carnegie, 36
Elizabeth Loftus, 10
George Orwell, 41
Melvil Dewey Story, 90
Nellie Bly, 77
Paul Vitz, 120
Stanton Samenow, 24
Viktor Frankl, 59
Walter Reed, 99
Grammar. *See* Errors, over-
coming
Group discussion, guidelines
for, 49–50, 51
Gullibility, 119, 120

Hasty conclusion, 126
Hazlitt, Henry, 147
Heimlich, Henry, 146
Honesty, 80

Ideas
assumptions and, 126–127,
128
examined, 11
producing, 80–81, 82
Imaginative, 75–76
Improvement, 66, 67
Individuality
definition of, 58
habits for developing,
79–83
influences on, 59–60, 62
Intelligence, 2–3
Internet
critical thinking and the,
193–194, 195
resource list and, 92–93
search engine and, 91–92.
See also Web sites
Interviews, 94, 95
Issues. *See* Arguments

Jordan, Michael, 18
Judgment
arguments and, 123
errors of, 9, 123–133, 194
ethical, 159–165
evidence and, 83
strategy for, 107

Kerry, John, 72
Kingsley, Charles, 155
Klein, Joel, 39
Knowledge
factual, 2
performance, 3
Kohn, Bob, 69
Korzybski, Alfred, 119

L'Amour, Louis, 11
Language, emotional, 70, 71
Lewinsky, Monica, 72
Library research, 89–90, 91
Loftus, Elizabeth, 10
Lubich, Chiara, 163

McGowan, William, 69
Magazines, 187–188
Mander, Jerry, 168, 176, 177
Manipulation

strategies to resist, 72–78
types of, 69–71, 72
Maurois, André, 154
Meaningless slogan, 168, 169
Mind, changing one's, 24–25,
26
"Mine is better" thinking, 118,
119
Minow, Newton, 175
Misleading statement, 170
Mistakes, 9, 10
Morris, Dick, 71
Movies
elements of, 183–184
explanation of critical
thinking and, 182
Music, 185–186

National Organization for
Women (NOW), 71
Navasky, Victor, 9
New York Times (newspaper),
69
Newspapers, 190–191
NOW. *See* National Organiza-
tion for Women (NOW)

Opinions
facts *vs,* 12–14
identifying, 101–103
Internet and, 193, 194
methods of testing, 16–19,
104
print journalism and,
191
Opportunities
in the classroom, 33
in the community, 34
in relationship, 34
in the workplace, 33, 34
Orwell, George, 41
Overgeneralizing, 124, 125
Oversimplification, 129

Peel, Robert, 16
Perception, errors in, 118–120,
194
Persuasion
achieving, 35–37, 38
advertising and, 173

definition of, 32
opportunities for, 33–34
Persuasive speaking
strategy for, 47–48.
See also Persuasion
Persuasive writing
strategy for, 38–41, 42.
See also Persuasion
Pisar, Samuel, 146
Plagiarism
avoiding, 95–96, 97
definition of, 95
Plot, 183
Popular culture, 62
Preparation, 72, 73
Pretending to know, 122
Pretenses, 122, 135, 136
Print advertising, 172–173
Problem solving
steps to, 147–149
unsatisfactory situation
and, 146
Proof, burden of, 134, 135
Published reports, 98

Questioning
errors and, 120
manipulation resistance
and, 73–74, 75

Reaction, errors of, 134–136,
194
Reason, 21–22
Reed, Walter, 99
Relationships
definition of, 150
dysfunctional, 151
guidelines for, 153–155
responsibility and, 152
types of, 151
Repetition, 72

Reports, published, 98
Research
arguments and, 105
reviews, 100, 101.
See also Internet
Respect
attitudes and, 68
of audience, 35
persuasion and, 37.
See also Ethical judgments
Rogers, Carl, 18

Samenow, Stanton, 24
Santayana, George, 16
Schlesinger, Arthur, Jr., 17
Schlessinger, Laura, 71
Scott, Arthur, 146
Search engine, 91
Selective perception, 119
Semmelweiss, Ignaz, 13
Setting, 183
Skepticism, 119, 120
Slogan, meaningless, 168, 169
Solutions, 148–149
Sources
checking, 78
library, 89–90, 91
Speaking. *See* Persuasive
speaking
Springboarding, 81
Stacking the deck, 71, 169
Statements, 13–14, 170, 194
Statistical studies, 100
Stereotyping, 124, 125
Straw man, 135, 136
Surveys, 100

Tavris, Carol, 83, 125
Television programming,
175–177
Testimonial, 169

Testimony, 98
Theme, 183, 184
"Therefore" relationships, 102
Thinking
definition and explanation
of, 4, 5
either/or, 122
errors in, 5
principles of, 5–11, 12
processes of, 4
strategy for, 26–27
Transfer, 169
Truth, discovered, 5–6

Viewpoints, 76, 82, 83
Vitz, Paul, 120
Voice-over, 169

Web sites
Aaron Feuerstein, 152
Albert Einstein, 3
career choices, 158, 159
checking rumors and
hoaxes, 78
Chiara Lubich, 163
errors in thinking on, 194
function of, 193
Google, 92
Melvil Dewey, 90
Nellie Bly, 77
resource list, 92–93
University of California at
Berkeley, 92
Walter Reed, 99
World Wide Web. *See* Internet;
Web sites
Writing. *See* Persuasive writing

Yochelson, Samuel, 24

About the Author

Vincent Ryan Ruggiero is an internationally known writer, lecturer, and consultant whose areas of special interest and expertise are critical and creative thinking, ethics, educational reform, and social criticism.

A pioneer in the movement to make thinking skills instruction an important emphasis at every level of education, he holds the rank of Professor Emeritus, State University of New York at Delhi, and resides in Dunedin, Florida.

Professor Ruggiero's twenty-one books include *Beyond Feelings: A Guide to Critical Thinking, Thinking Critically About Ethical Issues, The Art of Thinking, Teaching Thinking Across the Curriculum, A Guide to Thinking Sociologically, Warning: Nonsense Is Destroying America, Making Your Mind Matter,* and *The Practice of Loving Kindness.*